VITAL WORD STUDIES IN THE EPISTLE OF JAMES

VERSE-BY-VERSE, EXEGETICAL FORMAT

ΙΑΚΩΒΟΥ

ΕΡΙΣΤΟΛΗ ΚΑΘΟΛΙΚΗ

A Sound Scriptural Presentation
Based upon the Original Greek Test.

BY JOHN LINEBERRY

RoseDog✥Books
PITTSBURGH, PENNSYLVANIA 15238

The contents of this work including, but not limited to, the accuracy of events, people, and places depicted; opinions expressed; permission to use previously published materials included; and any advice given or actions advocated are solely the responsibility of the author, who assumes all liability for said work and indemnifies the publisher against any claims stemming from publication of the work.

RoseDog Books
585 Alpha Drive, Suite 103
Pittsburgh, PA 15238
Visit our website at www.rosedogbookstore.com

ISBN: 978-1-6376-4692-2
eISBN: 978-1-6376-4732-5

TABLE OF CONTENTS

PREFACE

The Epistle of James was written between 45 and 60 A.D., by James, the Lord's half-brother, Mat. 13:55; Mk. 6:3; Gal. 1:19), influential leader in the church at Jerusalem, Ac. 15:13), "A bond-servant of Jesus Christ."

Though addressed to the Jewish believers of the dispersion, the letter will be profitable for all believers. It is an inspired, integral portion of the Word of God, II Tim. 3:16.

The Epistle has as its general theme the outward evidence of the inward work of God in the soul, showing that the salvation of an individual manifests itself in living the Christian Life. The Holy Spirit empowers the child of God to magnify the Lord Jesus in daily, victorious living.

In reading the Scripture, one will observe that the Epistle of James does not conflict with the Epistle of Paul to the Romans. James has to do with justification before men, Jas. 2:14). Paul's teaching is about man's Justification before God (Rom. 3:24).

The Apostle Paul does not have in mind one kind of faith in saying that faith without works, saves, while James speaks of faith without works, does not save. "Both refer identically to the same kind of faith; namely, the faith that reaches out to trust Christ as Savior, resulting in the regeneration of the soul and Christian life (john 1:12).

The Greek words are transliterated into English. To illustrate: servant, 1:1, is (*doūlos), bond-servant, deō, tie, bind.* The child of God is bound eternally to the Lord Jesus by the unbreakable, cords of redemption, purchased by Calvary's love.

God, in salvation, lavishes, profusely, saving grace upon the believer (Eph. 2:8-9; Jas. 1:18).

Verb forms and function are distinguished. For example, the words in (5:12), *Swear not,* are present imperative in a prohibition which calls for the cessation of an action already in progress, *Stop swearing.*

Believers of the dispersion were swearing in ordinary conversation and exhorted to stop such practice. The Greek gives us added "golden nuggets" of truth.

The reader will find the Enlarged Translation helpful. It is placed at the end of each verse after comments and at the conclusion of the Letter. A fuller meaning is given to each verse as syntax permits. Standards Versions are held to a minimum of words in translation. Some riches, then, are left behind in the Greek text.

TRANSLATION

"Spiritually prosperous is the man who is constantly enduring temptation, because when he has been approved, he shall receive the crown of life, which He (the Lord) promised to those who are loving Him" Jas. 1:12.

Synonyms are distinguished, as in (chapter 4:1): *Wars (pólemos). Dispute. Quarrel.* Chronic state or campaign. *Fightings (máchai). Battle. Fight.* Single event.

THE EPISTLE OF JAMES
CHAPTER ONE

JAMES 1:1.

"James, a servant of God and of the Lord Jesus Christ, to the twelve tribes which are scattered abroad. Greeting."

GREETING AND SALUTATION

James is the inspired author, not the Apostle James, but the first pastor of the church at Jerusalem, and a faithful *bond-servant* of the Lord. The *bond-servant* has no agenda of his own but always seeks to do the will of the Lord in yielded, obedient devotion.

"*Of God and of the Lord Jesus Christ.*" Those words speak of the Father and the Son's equality in essence, power and worthy of worship. *God* refers to *the Father*. *Lord* is a designation of the *Son* who possesses every essence of diety. "*Fullness, Godhead, bodily*" (Col. 2:9).

Lord is often used in the Septuagint as the Hellenistic equivalent of *Jehovah* (Exod. 3:14). It is God's redemptive Name. God is also self-existent and eternal (John. 17:3). The Lord Jesus is the eternal Redeemer who delivers from death, ruin and sin. Thomas said to Christ, "My Lord and my God (John 20:28).

Jesus (Iēsoū, Matt. 1:21). Historical fulfillment of (Gen. 3:15), "And she shall bring forth a son, and you shall call His name JESUS: for He shall save His people from their sins."

There are three great truths in the word *Jesus:* (1) The deity of Christ; (2) His sinless humanity (Heb. 2:14); (3) His propitiatory sacrifice upon the Cross. Those truths are clearly in the Word (*Iēsoū*), because to save, our Lord must be God, sinless and die to settle the sin question.

Controversies have raged over the years about the humanity and deity of Christ: (1) Is Jesus like God? (2) Is Jesus God? Jesus is God (John 1:1).

Christ (Chrıstós). Anointed One (Chriō). Touch with the hand (Acts. 10:38). The O. T. prophet, priest and king were anointed with oil (Lev. 8:30). The *anointing* spoke of being empowered by the Holy Spirit to do the will of God in each respective office (Lev. 8:30).

The Lord Jesus was anointed with the Holy Spirit at the baptismal scene in the Jordan River (Matt. 3:16-17), as He began His public ministry to accomplish the ordained, redemptive plan of God as Prophet, Priest and King

A prophet speaks to man for God; a priest speaks to God for man; a king rules over man under God. The Hebrew equivalent of *Christ,* is the *Messiah.* The Lord Jesus is God's anointed Savior in whom alone is salvation, Ac. 4:12.

Twelve tribes (dōdeka phulaīs) were a synonym for the Jewish Nation. However, there was a marked distinction between Jews of the dispersion and Israeli Jews.

The *twelve tribes* refer to Israel in her fullness, for she is regarded as a unity (Acts. 26:7. Paul prayed for the whole nation (Rom. 10:1). *Scattered abroad (én tēi diasporāi), in the Dispersion.* It is the dative case of personal interest. God watches over His own (Ps. 125:1-2). The N. T. doesn't speak of any lost tribes.

Dispersion was used in the Septuagint of Israel dispersed among foreign nations (Deut. 28:25; 30:4), in Babylon (Jer. 25:11-12). First Peter 1:2 has in mind Christian Jews. Jews at this period were Palestinian Jews (agriculturists). Some other Jews were city dwellers and traders.

*Greetings (chaírein). Be rejoicing (*Phil. 4:4). The word is the usual Greek salutation: It was also used at parting: *Joy be with you* (Acts 15:23). Redemption brings heart peace and soul gladness so that the Christian, is able to rejoice in the ineffable blessings of grace, even amid trials.

TRANSLATION.

"James, of God and of the Lord Jesus Christ a bond-servant, to the twelve tribes, who are in the dispersion: Greetings"

James 1:2.

"My brethren, count it all joy when you fall into divers temptation."

Count, esteem (it) all joy (pāsan *chàran hēgēsasthe*). The words are placed first for emphasis. It is an unmixed joy (Phil. 2:29). Count it a thing wholly joyful, without admixture of sorrow. The pilgrim pathway is beset with many kinds of temptations, trails, though we can still have joy in victory.

You fall into (peripésēte). Fall into the midst of. The traveler from Jerusalem to Jericho "Fell among robbers" (Luke 10:30). Robbers had set a trap for him. Likewise, the tempter is ever alert to trip us up in the areas of: "Lust of the flesh, lust of the eyes, pride of life" (I John. 2:16).

My brethren (ádelphoí mou). From the same womb. Family. We are in the family of God. *Divers, (poikílois). Various. Temptations, peirasmoîs.* Temptations are any kind of distresses which come into our lives, from within or without.

(Peripésēte) is used exclusively of Satan who will test to see what evil is in us. Though temptations press upon the soul in harassing hostility, the child of God has inward joy in a world stricken with strife. Yielding continually to the Lord, we can have joy as we walk with the Lord.

Yielding to temptation is sin. Trials rightly faced, are harmless. The words, *(bear it);* (I Cor. 10:13), are from *(hupenegkeīn),* meaning that "God will provide a landing place," when we jump into His loving arms (Deut. 27:33;

TRANSLATION.

"*For yourselves, my brethren, count (*it) now, once and for all, all joy whenever you may fall into the midst of manifold trials*"

James 1:3.

"Knowing this, that the trying of your faith works patience."

Knowing (ginṓskō). Come to know is a discriminating apprehension of external impressions, knowledge grounded in personal experience. The word has a casual force, giving the reason for *Count it all joy* as a continual action in daily victory.

Trying (dokímion). In First Peter 1:7, the same word speaks of faith as genuine. Faith, like gold, stands the test of fire and is approved.

Definite article points to the special kind of faith. It is God-given faith, implanted in the heart by the Holy Spirit, enabling one to trust in and rely upon the Lord Jesus as Savior (John 6:29).

Faith, *písteōs trust.* It is the conviction God exists and is Creator, Ruler of all things, Provider, providing eternal salvation through Christ (Acts 4:12).

"In reference to Christ, faith is a strong and welcomed conviction that Jesus is the Messiah, (Anointed One), through Whom we are saved" (Acts 16:30-31).

Works (katergázetai). *Achieve. Perform.* Faith in the soul works successfully and thoroughly, for it keeps on working. *Patience (hupomonèn). Endure bravely.* Faith is the motivating principle of firmness and steadfastness. Faith is the victory! (I Cor. 15:58).

TRANSLATION.

"(May you), Constantly *(*be) *knowing by experience that the proving of your faith, is accomplishing endurance."*

> "Yield not to temptation,
> For yielding is sin;
> Each victory will help you
> Some other to win.
> "Fight manfully onward,
> Dark passions subdue;
> Look ever to Jesus,
> "He'll carry you through."
> —Palmer

James 1:4.

"But let patience have *her* perfect work, that you may be perfect and entire, wanting nothing."

Patience (hupomonè). Endurance. When believers were complaining about the mistreatment of pagan governors, Emperor Julian gave this sneer to them, "Bear it patiently as your God has commanded." Patience and Christian character were linked together. Is it much lacking today?

Perfect (téleioi) not sinless. Complete. With victory over impatience, the believer has reached the high plateau of maturity. Each resisting act, strengthens the child of God to trust Him for triumph over trials. *Work (*ergon). The Holy Spirit ministry in God's people.

Entire (holóklēroi). Finished. The perfect ones are mature (I Thess. 5:23), lacking in nothing. Maturity is the goal of patience.

TRANSLATION.

"But let endurance, the aforementioned one, be having (its) perfect (finished) work, in order that you may continually be mature, wholly complete and lacking nothing."

James 1:5.

"If any of you lack wisdom, let him ask of God, that gives to all *men* liberally, and upbraids not; and it shall be given him."

But if (eì dé). Fulfilled condition. Lack (leípetai). Destitute. (*vs.* 4 above). It is a banking term, denoting deficiency of funds." *Wisdom, sophía. Full intelligence.*

Wisdom is "The knowledge and practice of the requisite for godly and upright living," focusing on the Truth that we are to demonstrate outwardly what God's grace has made us inwardly.

Wisdom is operative in the believer's life for wise and best choices which honor God, seeking ever to do His will in thought, word and deed. Wisdom is recognized as expressing the highest and noblest, the practical use of knowledge. Some have identified *wisdom* as *goodness* itself.

Wisdom occurs in the New Testament as follows: wisdom: (1) The unsearchable wisdom of God (Rom. 11:33). *(2)* wisdom: supreme intelligence which belongs to Christ, exalted to God's right hand (Rev. 5:12); (3) wisdom which belongs to man (Luke 2:40).

Wisdom, in Paul's Epistles, is a knowledge of the divine plan previously hidden, providing salvation for men by the expiatory death of Christ at the Cross (I Cor. 1:30).

Let him ask (aíteitō). For something to be given. It is specific prayer, *Let him be asking.* Prevailing prayer is in view. The Lord wants us to ask and keep on asking. First Thessalonians 5:17 has it, "Be praying unceasingly." The pattern is: *Ask, seek, knock,* Matt. 7:7-8).

In prayer we also have fellowship with God (Num. 7:89; I John 1:3, 7. God is the greatest Giver. He delights to answer the prayers of His people. "O you that hears prayer, unto you shall all flesh come," Ps. 65:2. To gets one's prayers answered, puts new enthusiasm in the soul (John 15:7).

Liberally (haplōs). Generosity. Liberality shows the force of the word which lies in singleness of aim; namely, that the benefit is bestowed without requiring anything in return. Men often mar their giving by wrong motives.

Upbraids not (*mē óneidìzontos). Reproaches not.* It is subjective feeling rather than thought. There is a ring of contempt in the passage at the idea of a man with halting faith, expecting his prayers to be answered.

TRANSLATION.

"But if, as is the case, any of you be destitute of wisdom, let him be asking God Who is giving to all liberally and isn't reproaching, and it shall be given him."

James 1:6.

"But let him ask in faith nothing wavering. For he that wavers is like a wave of the sea driven with the wind and tossed."

Faith (pìstis). Confidence. Reliance. There is unlimited power in prayer. Seeking the will of God, is the initial thrust of prayer. There are many testimonies of answered prayer on the pages of Church History.

George Muller, (1805-1898), was a giant in prayer. He built an Orphanage in Bristol, England, which was sustained by prayers for many years. Torrey said, "Nothing lies outside the reach of prayer, except that which lies outside the will of God."

One who wavers in his faith, will not receive anything from the Lord (lēmpsis Kuríos). Christ (*vss.* 5:7, 14, 15). *Wavering (diakrinómenos). Doubting lit., to judge between,* going back and forth between belief and unbelief (Rom. 4:20). The doubting mind is the opposite of him who has unbending faith. The present tense indicates the believer, isn't ever to give over to doubting or hesitation. He must not vacillate between trust and distrust. *Like a wave of* the *sea (έoiken klúdōni thalássēs).*

The unstable Christian is pictured as one given over to doubting. Adam and Eve began their slipping, sliding downfall by doubting the goodness of God. They listened to the hissing lies of Satan.

For he that (ho gàr). Wavers (diakrinómenos). Doubting constantly is the culprit for unanswered prayer. The believer shouldn't let doubt get into the driver's seat.

Is like a w*ave (éoiken klúdōnizō). Dash. Surge.* It is a vivid picture of the instability of a billow, changing from moment to moment, is an apt symbol of a mind which cannot fix itself in trust.

Anyone who has watched a great ocean swell, throwing itself up into pointed waves, the tops of which are caught by the wind and fanned off into a spray, can surely appreciate the vivid picture.

Driven by the wind (ánemizoménōs). Tossed, hpizoménos). He is one whose mind wavers between hope and fear, doing and not doing.

The constant winds of doubt, may be deflected in the power of the Lord, for smooth sailing in prayer. However, one whose mind wavers in uncertain choices, delays spiritual growth to maturity, (II Pet. 3:18).

TRANSLATION.

*"But let him be asking in the sphere of faith, nothing doubting.
For he who is constantly doubting, is like a wave of the sea
continually driven by the wind and perpetually tossed about"*

James 1:7.

"For let not that man think that he shall receive anything of the Lord."

That man think (ho ánthrōpos ékeînos). Suppose. Will God answer the prayers of one storm-tossed about in his commitment? There is a ring of rebuke in the passage at the idea of a man, with halting faith, expecting answers.

Receive (lēpsetai). No one should be discouraged about prayer? However, one must walk before the Lord in yielded devotion in doing His will.

"For the LORD God *is* a sun and shield: the LORD will give grace and glory: no good thing will He withhold from them that walk uprightly" (Ps. 84:11; I John 3:22).

TRANSLATION.

"For let not that man be supposing that he shall receive anything from the Lord."

James 1:8.

"A double-minded man *is* unstable in all his way."

Man (ánēr). Individual man Double-minded (dipsuchos). Twice (dís). *Soul* (psuchē). A double-soul man is like Bunyan's "Mr. facing both ways." The soul is the seat of desire, self-consciousness, will. The individual is torn by conflicting desires.

How often Christians, though saved by grace unto good works, miss God's best in service, fail to count for Christ because torn and tossed about by divided desires. Being double-soul brings on instability and takes a high toll of effective service for the Lord.

Some bypass congregational harmony and sow seeds of discord (Phil. 2:2; 4:2). Some with the ability to serve and bless in a thrilling manner, starve out their soul by fretting, fuming and fussing.

Some who ought to edify, choose instead to neglect their part. Some who ought to be out battling the Devil in the power of God, are still in the baby stage of spiritual maturity.

U*nstable (ákatástatos). Fickle. Reels. Unreliable. In all his ways* (én pásais taḷís hodis aὐtoū). "It is a Hebrew expression, meaning his whole manner of life."

TRANSLATION.

"A double-soul man (torn by conflicting desires, (is) *unstable in all his ways (in his whole manner of life)."*

James 1:9.

"Let the brother of low degree rejoice in that he is exalted."

Low degree (ho tapeinòs). It is an outward condition (Luke 1:52); humble, poor (Ps. 9:39; Prov. 30:14). *Rejoice (kaucháomai). To glory.* The action follows the Lord's uplifting blessing.

Brother (*ádelphòs*). There is that closeness of fellowship among believers, for all believers are born of God (I Pet. 1:23). *Brother* shows that God is the Father of all believers, ruling out the slogan: "The brotherhood of man in a redemptive sense," an all inclusive mixture without Scriptural support (I Cor. 2:14).

Exalted (*tōi húpse aútoū*). *In his elevation.* In his low estate, he is in his elevation. "He that humbles himself shall be exalted" (Luke 4:11). The Christian brother's exaltation is a reality through his union with Christ, Head of the new creation (II Cor. 5:17).

The Christian is an "Heir of God and joint-heir with Christ," inheriting the "Riches of His grace" (Rom. 8:17; Eph. 1:7; 2:7; 3:8). "The meek shall inherit the earth" (Matt. 5:5).

TRANSLATION.

"But let the brother, the lowly one, be glorying in his exaltation."

James 1:10.

"But the rich, in that he is made low; because as the flower of the grass he shall pass away."

The rich *(ploúsios). Abundant, material resources.* Riches as such aren't sinful. The love of money is "The root of all kinds of evil" (I Tim. 6:10). The thought isn't money but the love of money.

Abraham was a wealthy man; yet, he was a man of faith (Rom. 4:3). Riches become evil when they stand between one and his Lord. Riches will give one a false security. "Riches are deceitful" (Matt. 13:22).

The Christian must follow always the simple rule of trusting God, at all times, for all things. Material benefits are to be used for the glory of God. Trouble soon ensues when earthly possessions control the believer, robbing him of communion with the Lord and usefulness in service.

The abounding brother, as well as the poor brother, should submit all to God, realizing that he is to be a faithful steward over that which has been committed to him (I Cor. 4:1-2).

A safe and good procedure for the Christian, with or without earthly wealth, to adhere to is, "Trust in the LORD with all your heart: and lean not unto your own understanding. In all your ways acknowledge him, and he shall direct your paths. Be not wise in our own eyes: fear the LORD, and depart from evil" (Prov. 3:5—7).

Claim daily the promise, "But my God shall supply all your need according to his riches in glory by Christ Jesus" (Phil. 4:19).

Made low (tapeinòs). Humiliation. "The Cross of Christ lifts up the poor and brings down the high. The Cross levels all men." *Flower (ănthos).* It is the bloom of the flower. *Grass (chórtos). Pasture. Fodder* (Mark. 6:34).

He shall pass away (pareleúsetai). He shall pass away completely from the earth. The warning is applied to the rich brother, but it is true of everyone
(Heb. 9:27).

TRANSLATION.

*"But the rich in his low estate (*humiliation*), because as the flower of the grass he shall pass away (*completely*)."*

James 1:11.

"For the sun is no sooner risen with a burning heat, but it withers the grass, and the flower thereof falls, and the grace of the fashion of it perishes, so also
shall the rich man fade away in his ways."

Is risen (*ànatéllō*). *To rise bodily.* The words are placed first for emphasis. The earlier Greeks used this word in reference to the rising of the sun and moon.

The b*urning heat (tōi kaúsōni).* The word is used with the article to denote something familiar to the recipients of the Epistle; namely, "The East wind from the Syrian desert. It was a burning heat, a hot wind which parched the vegetation and blighted the foliage of the trees."

And withers (kaì éxéranen). And dried up. Grass and flowers are used in the Word to show the ephemeral nature of life: "A step between me and death" (I Sam. 20:3).

Fall off (ékpíptō). Grace (eúprepeɩa). Goodly appearance. Beauty. Fashion (prosōpon). Face. Perishes (ápōleɩa). Destroyed. The flower is pictured as having a face, like a lily or rose. "The beautiful rose is pitiful when withered."

Rich man (ho ploúsios). Shall fade away (marainō). Extinguish a flame. His ways (poreíais). Journey. Like everyone else, the rich man's travel through life, will come to an end (Heb. 9:27). However, it is an uplifting truth that "We have an anchor of the soul both sure and steadfast" in the Lord (Heb. 6:19).

TRANSLATION.

"For the sun rises with the burning heat and dries up the grass and its flower falls off, and the beauty of its appearance perishes; so also the wealthy (man) in his goings (pursuits) shall wither (away)."

James 1:12.

"Blessed *is* the man that endures temptation: for when he is tried, he shall receive the crown of life, which the Lord has promised to them that love him."

Blessed (makários). Happy. Prosperous. It is spiritual prosperity. The word is used in the Beatitudes (Matt. 5:1-12). Heaven is the depository of true treasuries which cannot be stolen nor corrupted by decay. *Man (ánēr). Particular man.*

Endures trials (hupoménō). Abide under. Bear bravely. Calmly. Continuous action. The believer doesn't endure to be saved, but endures because he is saved. Remaining steadfast against temptation, under all circumstances in the power of the Lord, brings reward to the child of God (I Cor. 3:11—15).

Temptation (peirasmón). It is the process of putting one to the test to see what good or evil is in a person. The solicitous, suggestions of Satan, are highlighted.

This type of temptation is used most frequently in a hostile sense. Now, the word is understood of testing or trying intentionally to see what evil is in a person. The Devil tests to disapprove.

Another word, tried, (dókimos), is to test to approve. God tests to approve. Another word, (ádókimos), means to disapprove, disqualified for service (I Cor. 9:27). Waywardness in a Christian's life, will disqualify him for service.

The crown (tòn stéphanon). The victor's crown. It is an award given to the believer in recognition of victory over temptations. This crown isn't eternal life. He has that already, or he could not have overcome temptations.

Furthermore, this is a crown given to a believer for what he has done, whereas salvation is a free gift, in view of what Christ did on the Cross (John 1:12-13; 19:30).

Of life (tēs zōēs). The life. The eternal life the believer has in Christ, enables him to overcome temptations through the ministry of the Holy Spirit.

Has promised (ἐpēggeílato). Announce. To them that (toĩs). To those who.

Dative case brings out God's special love for His people who are constantly tested by the Devil. His wicked promptings to sin, are met successfully and overcome by the Lord's enabling grace, proving, thereby, their love for the Savior, winning the uplifting, approbation of the Master.

Love Him (ágapōsin aútón). Loving Him. This is God's love implanted in our heart at the moment of salvation. It is the love called out of the heart of the Lord for the preciousness of the object loved. It is God's, self-sacrificing love manifested at the Cross.

It is God's manifested love for mankind (John 3:16); the love which God is in His essential nature (I John 4:8); the love shed abroad in our hearts by the Holy Spirit (Rom. 5:5). The ingredients of God's love are in (I Cor., chap. 13).

TRANSLATION.

"Spiritually prosperous is the man who is constantly enduring temptation, because when he has been approved, he shall receive the crown of life which He (the Lord) promised to those who are loving Him."

James 1:13.

"Let no man say when he is temped, I am tempted of God: for God cannot be tempted with evil, neither tempts he any man."

No man (mēdeìs). No one. Tempted, peirazō). To lust. Let say légō). Speak. That from God (hóti apò toũ Theoũ). It is wicked, indeed, for one to blame God for his sins. *For God is not to be tempted by evils (ho gár Theòs éstin àpeirastós kakōn). And He Himself tempts no one (aútòs peirázei dè oúdéna).*

Alford said, "God ordains the temptation, over rules the temptation, but does not tempt, is not the spring of solicitation to sin." God at times does test man in order to show man his sinfulness and develop his character.

TRANSLATION.

"(When) being tempted, let no one be saying, From God as a source, I am being temped, for God is incapable of being

tempted by things evil in nature; indeed, He Himself is tempting no one."

James 1:14.

"But every man is tempted, when he is drawn away of his own lust, and enticed."
Every man (hékastos). Each one. Separately. Of (hùpò). *By. Agency. Lust* (épithumía). *Craving. Desire.* The context will determine the meaning, if good or bad. It is evil here as in (Rom. 7:7). It is used in a good sense in (Phil. 1:23).

Lustful cravings originated in man himself. "The heart is deceitful above all *things,* and desperately wicked *incurably sick" (*Jer. 17:9).

Drawn away (éxelkō). To draw out from within. Robertson commented, "The word is taken from hunting and fishing. As game is lured from it covert, so man by lust is allured from the safety of self-restraint to sin." Lust hounds man's footsteps, doggedly.

Enticed (deleázō). Bait. Catch. Beguile. Deceive. Drawn way and enticed describe the working of lust. The thrust of temptation is to draw man out of his repose and allured him to a bait.

Drawn away was used of fishing; enticed was used of hunting. Satan seeks to pull us out of the pathway of righteousness and then shoots us down with his fiery darts (Eph. 6:10—17). He will fail of his intent, however, since there is triumph in Christ (I John 5:4-5).

TRANSLATION.

"But each one is being tempted by his own (lustful) desire, when he is being drawn away and is being enticed."

James 1:15.

"Then, when lust has conceived, it brings forth sin; and sin when it is finished, brings forth death."

Has conceived (sullaβoūsa). The will yields to lust and conception takes place. *Brings forth (tíktō). Bear. Produce.* Lustful desires cause much heartache and slays a lot of people, disrupting marital tranquility like a ferocious lion.

Sin (hē harmartía). The Sin is missing the mark of God's glory (Rom. 3:23). The article highlights the nature of sin. The pull of lust is sinful desire. Sin is the union of the will with lust.

Finished (ápotelestheīsa). Complete. In every detail. Sin at birth is fully equipped for its nefarious career (Rom. 6:6; Gal. 3:5). *Brings forth (ápokúei). From the womb.* Sin has a continuous, powerful effect upon those who submit to its allurements.

Death (*thánaton*). Death is the temporary suspension of the spirit and soul from the body, bringing an end to life on earth. There will be a reunion of the spirit and soul with the body (Eccles. 12:7; I Cor. 15:54; I Thess. 4:13-18).

TRANSLATION.

"Then the (lustful) desire having conceived, is bringing forth sin, the (aforementioned) sin having been fully completed is giving forth to death."

James 1:16.

"Do not err, my beloved brethren."

Err (planaō). Lead astray. "Stop being deceived." The way of sin is to deceive and kill (Rom. 7:7—14). The Devil delights in blinding man's eyes about sin and its consequences (Rom. 1:27; II Cor. 4:4; Eph. 4:14). *Beloved (ágapētos). Divinely-loved ones. Brethren (ádelphoi).* There is blessed oneness in Christ.

TRANSLATION.

"Stop being deceived, my brethren, divinely-loved ones."

James 1:17.

"Every good gift and every perfect gift is from above, and comes down from the Father of lights, with whom is no variation, neither shadow of turning."

Good (ágathè). *Good in kind. Gift* (dósis). *Free. Large (dōrēma) (Rom. 5:16).* The verbal from expresses an act of giving. *Perfect* (téleion). It shows the moral quality of the gift. Reaching out to someone, is an emotional uplift.

From above (ănōthen). Father of lights (toū Patròs tōn phōtōn). "The statement that these gifts are from God, is in the pursuance of the idea that God doesn't tempt man to evil."

The gifts of God are contrasted with the evil springing from man's lust." God is the Giver of every good gift (John 3:16). *From above (ănōthen)*. *Heaven* (John 3:31). The inherent quality of the gift is by its very nature, sent down from above, from God. *Comes down (katabaīnon)*.

The seasons may change but the Lord's providential care of us, is constant. The gifts of His grace, are demonstrations of God's abounding love and limitless mercy toward us.

"I will sing of the mercies of the LORD forever: with my mouth will I make known your faithfulness to all generations" (Ps. 89:11).

From the Father (àpò toū Patròs). *From. Ultimate source.* The benefits of God's grace come not from the merits of man but from our heavenly Father, Creator of all things (Job 38:28). God is the Author of light and lights, the Father of those fountains of light (Gen. 1:3, 14—18).

Of lights (tōn phōtōn). *Heavenly bodies.* God is "The Father of lights," Creator and Sustainer (Ps. 8:3; Amos 5:8). Beyond the mention of the heavenly bodies, the context surely means God is also the Creator of spiritual light. Jesus is "The true light" (John 1:9; 8:12).

What refreshing comfort to know the Lord Jesus as personal Savior; to walk with Him, ever ordering our life within the environs of His light.

We now possess eternal life through the exercise of God-given faith in the finished work of Christ at the Cross, and hence are safe from the world's confusion, darkness and doom.

Variableness (parallagē). *Change.* The word isn't used in an astronomical, technical sense as supposed by some but in the ordinary meaning of change. The change is that uncertainty of degree of light which we see in the material, heavenly bodies, but which isn't in God the Creator.

Shadow (àposkíasma). *A shade cast by* one object on *another. Turning (tropē)*. *Occasion. Cause.* Shadow of turning is popularly understood to mean that there isn't the faintest hint or shade of change like the shadow of suspicion.

The Revised Version has "Shadow that is cast by turning," referring still to the heavenly orbs, which cast shadows in their revolution, as when the moon turns her dark side to us, or the sun is eclipsed by the body of the moon.

"There is no such periodic variation in God like that we see in the heavenly bodies." "For I *am* the LORD, I change not" (Mal. 3:6).

TRANSLATION.

"Every good gift and every perfect gift is from above, coming down from the Father of lights (heavenly bodies), with whom there is no variation, (change), nor shadow cast by turning."

James 1:18.

"Of his own will beget he us with the word of truth, that we should be a kind of first fruits of his creatures."

Will (βoulḗtheìs). The word speaks of the rational side, for the choice was deliberate. God the Father acted of a set purpose in causing us to become recipients of His grace in salvation.

The tense shows the fact of the deliberate choice of God in past time in designating us to receive the ministry of the Holy Spirit, Who uses the Word to bring about regeneration.

Begat (ἀpekúēsen). *Bring from the womb.* The word is used in *(vs.* 15 above). The gift of elective grace is effected by regeneration (John 3:3, 5).

With the Word (lógōı) which means *thought, reason* who; therefore is a person. It is used of Christ in (John 1:1). Christ is the living Word and possesses fullest deity. *God was the Word (Theòs ēn ho Lógos). Christ.*

The instrumental case, the case of means, *by means of the Word.* The Word is made alive by the Holy Spirit in the heart of the believer. Salvation is a work of God for man, not a work of man for God.

Of Truth (álētheías). Genitive of description: *Word marked by Truth.* The Word of Truth is the gospel, the power of God unto salvation (Rom. 1:16).

Your Word is Truth (John 17:17); the gospel (I Cor. 4:15; 15:1-4), the Word of God and the Word of the Lord (I Pet. 23—25). The Word reaches our heart, showing us our need of salvation.

First fruits (áparchē). The figure is taken from Christ and salvation (Rom. 1:16; Eph. 1:12). Jewish, law requirements were that the first-born of men, cattle, and the first growth of fruits and grain, should be consecrated to the Lord.

The lesson in the illustration, is that Christians, as first fruits, should be consecrated to God (Rom. 12:1-2). First fruits are common in the N.T.: of the Spirit (Rom. 8:23); Christ in the resurrection (I Cor. 15:20).

Born the first time, we become members of Adam's dying race (Rom. 5:12).

The second birth places us in God's living family (Eph. 3:14—16). The Holy Spirit makes alive the Word of God in the soul, taking us from death to life, darkness to light (John 6:63; Col. 1:12-14).

His (aútoū). God becomes our Father in redeeming us "By His precious blood" (I Pet. 1:19). *Creatures (ktísma).* Christians are God's peculiar possession. We aren't only His by creation, but also His by right of redemption (I Cor. 6:19—20; Tit. 2:14). *First fruits* means a bigger harvest will come.

TRANSLATION.

"Because He (God) deliberately willed it. He gave to us a (spiritual) birth by means of (the) Word of Truth, resulting in our being a kind of first fruits of His creatures."

TRANSLATION.

James 1:19.

"Wherefore, my beloved brethren, let every man be swift to hear, slow to speak, slow to wrath."

Born into the family of God, the child of God is called upon to be on the outside in his daily behavior what he is by grace on the inside. *Swift (tachús).* Quick. The word is found in a papyrus writing in the following sentence, translated by the word *quickly.* "It is well for him to come *quickly,* for he will instruct you."

Hear (ákoūsai). Attend to. The word embraces the whole business of hearing. The word clears the way for a proper reception of the saving Word of God.

Slow (βradùs). It means slow to begin speaking, not slow while speaking. *To speak (tò lalēsai). Substance* In a broader concept, denotes to be eager to listen, not eager to discourse.

Wrath often leads to an outburst of temper, found in the wake of a swift rejoinder and ready chattering. In many cases, one may say more by saying less.

"A soft answer turns away wrath, but grievous words stir up anger. The tongue of the wise uses knowledge aright, but the mouth of fools pours out foolishness"

(Prov. 15:1-2). *Wrath (órgēn). Speak slowly* when angry. *Slow to anger (βradòs eís órgēn).*

Anger has been defined, "As a moment of insanity." This recognition might help in curbing anger. *Wrath (órgēn).* It arises gradually and becomes more settled." *Passion (thumós).* It boils up and then subsides.

Wrath (òrgē) when used of God, has reference to that in God which stands opposed to man's disobedience, stubbornness, especially in resisting the gospel. God's wrath manifests itself in punishment of those who reject Christ. Summary: intemperate talking leads to wrath.

TRANSLATION.

"You know absolutely, my beloved brethren! Now, let every man practice being quick to hear, slow to speak, slow to wrath and slow to anger."

James 1:20.

"For the wrath of man works not the righteousness of God."

Wrath (órgē). Righteousness (δικαιοσύnē). Righteous in God's sight (I Cor. 1:30; Phil. 3:9). *God (Theós).* God provides this righteousness.

"How many an endeavor, which might have ended in working out the righteousness of God among us, has been blighted, diverted by hasty speaking and anger, end in disgracing ourselves, and Him Whom we would have served, before men."

"Man's wrath is rarely justifiable, even in just indignation, because, often, it is mixed with other elements, which are founded upon false premises." Man, unlike God, doesn't know all the circumstances. Lacking the facts, we come up short and embarrass ourselves.

TRANSLATION.

"For man's wrath does not result in that which is righteous in the sight of God."

James 1:21.

"Wherefore lay apart all filthiness and superfluity of naughtiness, and receive with meekness the engrafted word, which is able to save your souls."

Wherefore (*dió*). *On which account. Lay apart (*àpothémenoi*). Put off from.* The word is used in a sentence: "To put off and away from one's self. The tense speaks of a single, decisive act."

*Filthiness (*hruparían*). Moral defilement.* "The filth of the flesh" is seen in (I Pet. 3:2). Evil will occupy the heart if care isn't taken to root it out.

*Superfluity (*perisseían*). Abundance. Naughtiness (kakía). Evil. Ill-will.* It is evil in the abstract. Evil (*ponēris*). Evil is seen in its active opposition to the good and is descriptive of Satan in his wicked activity against God. *Malice (kakía). Vice. Receive (dechomai). Appropriate. With meekness (én poiētes). In meekness.*

*Doers (*poiētēs*). Performer.* It is the old word for agent (*poieō*), to do as in (Romans 2:13), but in (Acts 17:28), poet, long regarded as a doer or maker.

Salvation in the soul results in good works in the life. The Lord saves us to serve: "Walk in good works" (Eph. 2:10); "Zealous of good works" (Tit. 2:14); "Be careful to maintain good works" (Tit. 3:8). There are too many "lily Christians" in our churches. They neither "toil nor spin."

*Deceiving (*paralogizómenoi*). Cheat. False reasoning. Your one word* (heautous). The man who hears without doing, doesn't hook-wink anyone but himself.

TRANSLATION.

"Now, keep on becoming doers of the Word and not hearers only, constantly cheating yourselves by false reasoning."

James 1:23.

"For if any be a hearer of the word, and not a doer, he is like a man beholding his natural face in a glass."

For (hóti). Because. If (eí). Fulfilled condition. If, assuming that, if, as is the case. There were some believers, as today, who merely listened to the gospel message, but failed to put it into daily, godly living. The light of right doctrine needs to shine with right living.

Beholding (katanoéō). Consider attentively. Man takes a studied gaze at himself but leaves without making any change at all. *Natural face (prósōpon). Face of his birth.* It is one's origin, lineage, nativity. *In a glass* (*ésótpōı*). *Mirror.*

Robertson stated, "The mirrors of the Ancients were made of polished metals, usually of copper, silver and tin. The word of God is a mirror in which we may and ought to see our moral countenance."

TRANSLATION.

"Because if, assuming that, anyone is hearing the Word and not a doer, this one is like a man attentively considering the face of his birth in a mirror."

James 1:24.

"For he beholds himself, and goes his way, and straight way forgets what manner of man he was."

He beholds (katenóēsen). Fix one's eyes upon. The verb shows that the man takes a single look, and soon forgets what he saw. *Goes his way (ápelēluthen). Go off.* The perfect tense denotes enduring results. Off *he has gone* with the present result, he is still away.

Straightway (eútheōs). Immediately. Forget. (épelátheto. He forgot completely. *What manner of man he was (hopoîos). What sort.* Perhaps, James is describing an actual case that occurred in the past.

One authority commented. "The man took notice and went away. He forgot what kind of man he was. All of it just dropped out of his mind. Yes, he came and heard again and again, but this was the story every time." Is this not a picture of the average Church-goer?

He who remains untouched by the dynamic power of the gospel, misses out on blessings from Heaven. This is a vivid, life-like picture, of the careless listener to preaching.

TRANSLATION.

"For he takes a look at himself and off he has gone, and immediately, completely forgot what sort of man he was."

James 1:25.

"But whosoever looks into the perfect law of liberty, and continues *therein,* he being not a forgetful hearer, but a doer of the work, this man shall be blessed in his deed."

But he that (*ho dè*). It is a contrast between the doer and non-doer. *Looks* (*parakúptō*). *Bow the head. Bend forward.* The word speaks of one who stoops sideways for a better look. It was used of John and Mary, *stooping down* (John 20:5;20:11).

The angels desire to look into the glories of the gospel. Metaphorically, the word means to look into carefully, augmented by eagerness and concentration (I Pet. 1:12).

Into (*eís*). It was a look into the very essence of the Law. Without the article nature and quality are stressed (*éleutherías*). *Word of Truth (vs.* 1:21). *Implanted. Perfect* (*téleion*). *Completeness. Law* (*nómos*).

The use of the article, (*tēs*), points to a particular Law of Liberty, and introduces a limitation, defining that perfect Law to be the Law of Liberty.

"The freedom of the Law in Christ is contrasted with the minute working that characterized the development of the Mosaic system."

"The Law in Christ, then, is called a perfect Law because it is final and complete, as distinct from the Mosaic Law which was transitory."

It is called the *Law of Liberty* because it rests upon the finished work of Christ, whose Truth sets us free (John 8:32, 36; Rom. 8:1; II Cor. 3:16). Since the *Law of Liberty* is anchored upon Christ's redemptive ministry; it is perfect, lacking nothing for completeness. *Continues* (*parameínas*). *Remain beside.*

Having not been a forgetful hearer (*genómenos (oúk epílēsmonē ákroatēs*). This person submits to the Word of God as the Holy Spirit brings forth Christ-likeness into our life and soul (II Pet. 3:18). But a doer (*allà poiētēs*). *Of the work* (*érgon*).

Blessed (*makários*). *Spiritual prosperity. In his deed* (*én tēi poiēsei autoū*). *In his doing. In (én).* It marks the connection between doing and blessing. The joy of this humble, active Christian, is like the wise man at the end of The Sermon on the Mount, "Who built his house upon a rock" (Matt. 7:24-25). "The life of obedience is the element wherein blessedness is found .

TRANSLATION.

"He who has carefully looked into the perfect Law, the Law of Liberty, and has always continued (in it), not having become a hearer of forgetfulness but a doer of work, this man shall be blessed (spiritually) in his doing."

James 1:26.

"If any man among you seem to be religious, and bridles not his tongue, but deceives his own heart, this man's religion *is* vain."

If (eí). Fulfilled condition. Any man (tıs). Anyone. Seem (dokéō). Opinion. Think. Religious (thrēskeía). "The focus is on external observances of public worship: such as church attendance, alms giving, prayer, fasting" (Matt. 6:1—18).

Bridles (chalınagōgōn). *Lead.* It also means to hold in check, restrain. The picture is that of a man, putting a bridle in his mouth to harness his tongue.

Tongue (glōssan). An uncontrolled, unbridled tongue, causes much, irreparable harm. *Wisdom (sophía). Instructs. Put a knot on your tongue.* God hates "A lying tongue" (Prov. 6:17).

The tongue of the Christian is to be exercised in "Speaking the truth in love" (Eph. 4:15); "To speak truth with his neighbor" (Eph. 4:25). A believer must not allow his tongue to engage in corrupt communication, but take the high road of grace to edify one another along the Pilgrim path (Eph. 4:29).

But (áll'). Stronger negation. Deceives (ápatōn). Cheat. Beguile. Another word *(ápataō). Trick. Stratagem.* The person who doesn't hold his tongue in check, is just playing a trick on himself, programmed in self-deception.

His (heautón). It is a reflexive pronoun, showing that the person who supposes he is religious without restraining his tongue, is himself the object of being cheated in these matters. *Heart (kardía). Affections. Desires,*

This man (toútos). This one. Serving the Lord acceptably, pleasingly, must be preceded by salvation in the soul, brought about by God-given faith in the finished work of Christ upon the Cross (II Cor. 5:19-20). *Vain (mátaios). Worthless. Useless.*

TRANSLATION.

"If, assuming that, anyone supposes himself to be religious, not bridling his tongue but deceiving his own heart, this man's religion is useless."

James 1:27.

"Pure religion and non-defiled before the Father is this, to visit the fatherless and windows in their affliction and to keep himself without spot from the world."

Pure (katharà). Clean. Undefiled (ámíanos). Religion (thrēskeía). Religion is "External, religious worship, treated in (vs. 25 above)." Robertson said, "There are numerous examples in the papyri (writing material) and inscriptions of *(thēskeía),* pertaining to religion for-ritual and reverential worship in the Roman Empire."

Before our God (parà tōi Theōi). Before. By the side of. Father (Patrì). From God's standpoint, Pure and non-defiled religion, will manifest itself in doing service for the Lord. God knows about the thoughts of our heart and labor of our hands.

To visit. (épisképtesthai). Go see. There is an emotional dynamic in it! *The fatherless (órphanoùs). Widows (chēras) (*Matt. 25:36, 43). *In their affliction (én tēi thlípsei). Pressing together. Tribulation. Distress.* Widows and Orphans have a special need.

To keep. (tēreō). Watchful care. The Christian is to be alert and watchful for hidden pitfalls along the way. un*spotted (ǎspilon). Unsullied.* Oneself (*heautòn*). *Away from (ápò). The world (toū kósmou).* It is used with the ablative, the case of separation.

The believer must keep himself continually off and away from the world's corruption and sin. The world is "The whole earthly creation, separated from God and lying in sin, which, whether considered as in the men who serve it or alluring enticements to evil."

The world is a source of continual defilement for believers. However, believers, are separated from the world; yet, at the same time, we are in the world. *Lust (épithumía). Lurking. Entice. Pollute.* We need to be diligent, therefore, to keep ourselves off the path of *Lust* (I Tim. 6:14).

"The LORD watches over the way of the righteous, but the way of the wicked will perish" (Ps. 1:6). The believer has victory through faith in Christ (I John 5:4). "This keeping is, indeed, in the higher sense, God's work (John 17:5); but it is also our work." "Keep yourself pure" (I Tim. 5:22).

TRANSLATION.

"Religion (which is) pure and unsoiled before God, even the Father is this: to visit and look after Orphans and Widows in their distress, (and) practice keeping one's self from the world."

CHAPTER TWO

James 2:1.

"My brethren, have not the faith of our Lord Jesus Christ, the Lord of glory, with respect of persons."

My brethren (ádelphoi mou). Fellow believers. All believers are born of God through the ministry of the Holy Spirit (John 1:13; 3:3, 5). *My (mou).* There is a relationship between James and his readers who are his brethren in Christ by the bond of grace.

Have not (mē 'échete). Hold. The syntax here with *(mē)* in the present imperative, shows a practice already in progress, forbidding its continuance. S*top holding. Hold* best suits the context.

Faith (pístis). It is clearly objective genitive, not subjective, not *faith of* but *faith in* our Lord Jesus Christ. *Lord of glory (tēs doxēs). Christ's deity.*

Faith is here as in (Galatians 2:16); namely, "The acceptance of that which accredits itself as true, and a corresponding trust in the person concerning whom the facts are presented." God-given faith leads one to trusts Jesus as personal Savior (John 6:29).

Our (hēmōn). Believers belong to the Lord by right of redemption. *Lord* (Kurios). Our God is the sovereign Lord of the universe. *Jesus (Iēsoū).* Translation of the Hebrew *Joshua, God saves.*

(Matthew 1:21), historical fulfillment of Genesis 3:15 states, "And she shall bring forth a son, and you shall called his name Jesus: for he shall save his people from their sins." God does all the saving of a soul (Mark 10:45; Luke 19:10).

Salvation is an eternal work of God, permanent and unchangeable (Eccles. 3:14). To save the Lord Jesus possesses: deity, sinless humanity, died on the Cross to settle the sin question. He is "Very God of very God.

Christ (Christos). The Anointed One. Hebrew Messiah (Acts 10:38). *Of glory (tēs doxēs).* The words refer to the Lord Jesus. The glory is the Shekinah glory of God (John 17:5; II Cor. 4:6; Heb. 1:3).

With (én). In connection with. Respect of persons (prosōpolēmpteite) (Not) *To receive one's face* or *countenance* (Lev. 19:15; Luke 20:21; Rom. 2:11; Jude 1:16). *Impartial.*

"Of a truth I perceive that God is no respecter of persons" (Acts 10:34). God accepts no one's face. He looks on the heart (I Sam. 16:7). How inconsistent with the Christian because of his position in Christ and testimony, to show overt acts of partiality. The Brethren are exhorted to stop showing partiality of persons.

TRANSLATION.

"Mr brethren, stop holding the faith in our Lord Jesus Christ, (the Lord) of the glory in connection with showing partiality to persons."

James 2:2.

"For if there come unto your assembly a man with a gold ring, in good apparel, and there come in also a poor man in vile raiment."

If (éàn). It is the particle used with the subjunctive and presents a hypothetical situation. *Come (eíselthuí. To enter. Assembly (sunagōgēn). Bring together. Place of worship. Man (ànèr). Individual man.*

With a gold ring (chousodaktúlıos). Adorned with a gold ring. It is a picture of a man who has his hands loaded with rings and jewels. A ring was regarded as an indispensable article of Hebrew attire. The ring contained his signet.

Name of the ring (Tabbame). Impress a seal. It was a proverbial expression for a most, valued object (Isa. 22:24; Hag. 2:23).

The Greeks and the Romans wore rings in great profusion. Hannibal, after the battle of Canna, sent a trophy to Carthage, three bushels of gold rings from the finger of the Roman Knights, slain in battle.

It was said of Charínus that he wore six rings on each finger never laid them aside at night or when bathing. Among rings found in the catacombs, are some with a key, and some with both key and seal, for both locking and sealing a casket.

Goodly (lamprāi). Shining. Brilliant. Apparel (esthēti). Poor man (ptōchos). Beggarly mendicant (Matt. 19:21). *In vile (en hruparāi). Dirty. Filthy.*

The believer needs a proper attitude toward the rich and poor, being careful to abstain from partiality in his associations.

TRANSLATION.

"For if there comes into your synagogue (meeting place for Christian Jews), a man with a gold ring on his hand in shining clothing, and there comes also a poor, beggarly man in dirty clothing."

James 2:3.

"And you have respect to him that wears gay clothing, and say unto him, sit you here in a good place; and say to the poor, stand you here, or sit at my footstool."

You have respect (épιβlépsēte). Turn eyes upon. The thought is to look with respectful consideration or to look with admiration. *Wear (phoreō).* (Matt. 11:8). In this situation, carnality is popping up all over the place.

Sit (káthou). As for you, be sitting down. Here (hōde). Seat of honor. One authority is of the opinion the places of honor, were the first seats in the synagogue. Elders and Scribes liked honor seats.

May come in also (eísélthēi). *Poor (man) (ptōchēí). In vile apparel. (hruparâi). You Stand (Sú stēthou). As for you, take a stand in that place. Footstool (tò. hupopódιón). Beside me. Seat of disgrace. Shame.*

With drained emotions, the man's heart was ripped apart. "He that has mercy on the poor, happy is he" (Prov. 14:21). "The righteous considers the cause of the poor" (Prov. 29:7).

"Blessed, *(spiritually prosperous),* are the poor for theirs is the kingdom of heaven" (Matt. 5:3). The poor, as citizens of the Kingdom of Heaven, we must reach out to them.

What a place of honor for the well-to-do gentleman as he takes his seat of class. So much so James asks, "Are you Christians still impressed by a gold ring and a bright attire?"

But to the poor man has no respect shown to him at all. He is told to stand there by the wall or wherever he can be wedged in, in the back. It is gross unfairness.

No one would think of treating the rich visitor in that manner. Oh! No! That is the point James makes. His readers are still respecters of persons in the evil sense of the word. It is also a common problem in our day and needs to be corrected.

TRANSLATION.

"And you look with admiration upon the one wearing the shining clothing and say, as for you, be sitting down here in this seat of honor and say to the poor, beggarly (man), as for you, take a stand in that place or be sitting down beside my footstool."

James 2:4.

"Are you not then partial in yourselves, and are become judges with evil thoughts?"

Partial (diekríthēte). Yourselves (heautoĩs). Not (ou). Become judges (diakrinō). Judge between. Discriminate. Are you not divided in you own mind?

Their behavior is contrary to the faith, they professed.

Are (gínomai). Have become. Judges (kritaì). Of evil (ponēros). Pernicious. Evil activity. Opposed to the good. Thoughts (dialogismōn). To Reason. The evil thoughts are in the judges themselves and consist of the undue preference given to the rich. Stop showing partiality!

The judges were engaged in the same activity as busybodies. A busybody is a self-appointed overseer in the affairs of others (I Peter 4:15).

TRANSLATION.

"Are you not divided in your own mind and have become judges with wicked thoughts"?

James 2:5.

"Hearken, my beloved brethren, Has not God chosen the poor of this world to be rich in faith and heirs of the kingdom which he has promised to them that love him"?

Hearken (ἀkouō). Listen. Attend to. Alford said, The words, "Hearken, my beloved brethren," are one of the few links which connect the Epistle with the speech of James in Jerusalem (Acts 15:13). God *(Theòs). God the Father. Chosen (éxeléxato). Choose. Pick out.* The verbal, middle voice, shows God chose for Himself those who would be His elect and receive His efficacious grace.

In salvation God the Father selects the believer (Eph. 1:4); God the Son saves (Eph. 1:7); and God the Holy Spirit seals the believer (Eph. 1:13). The ground of God's elective grace in salvation, is based, solely on the Cross of Christ, not anything the believer is or has done.

Election (I Thess. 1:4; II Thess. 2:13). *The Poor (tous ptōchoès).* "By using the article *(tous),* James doesn't affirm God chose all the poor, but only that He did choose poor people"(Matt. 10:23—26; I Cor. 1:26—28).

Of this world (toūs kósmou). World's system. The Poor are "Those who in this world's estimation, are accounted poor." The world's pernicious system, is in view (I John 5:19). This present world is headed up by Satan (Eph. 2:2). The world gropes in the throes of corruption: economically, politically, religiously, socially. The child of God isn't in this world's passing parade.

Rich in faith (plousíou én pístgs). Treasures of salvation. "We are children, heirs, joint-heirs with Christ" (Rom. 8:17). Chafer said, "At the moment of salvation, thirty-three blessings of God's grace, are given to the believer."

True, permanent, abundant wealth consists of spiritual possessions—things of God and Heaven—not the decaying, dying, fleeting, perishable things of this earth. The believer, therefore, is now and forever spiritually prosperous (Eph. 1:3).

Faith (pístis). Trust. Reliance. Confidence. Our trust in and reliance upon, augmented by confidence, is in the Lord Jesus, Lord of glory, Who died for us at Calvary, provided for the eternal safety of our souls in salvation from sin, deliverance from death and redemption from ruin (John 3:16-17).

The believer's God-given faith is in Christ as Savior. Faith may be defined as a personal, full-fledged trust in Christ for salvation, from sin's consequences, power (Rom. 6:23).

Heirs (klēronómous). Receive by lot. Kingdom, the Messianic, Millennial Kingdom of Christ, when He shall rule over the nations with a rod of iron in fulfillment of the prophetic Scriptures; namely, the unfailing promises of God to His people (Ps. 2:9; Dan. 2:44; Luke 1:32-33; Rev. 19:15; 20:4, 6). In that Kingdom, we shall reign, along with Israel, with Christ on the throne of His glory (Matt. 19:28).

He has promised (épagellō). Announce. The fuller thought is to announce that which one is about to do or finish something. God of His own will, promised blessings of His Kingdom, according to His own glory and good pleasure, not according to anything deserving in us.

The promises of God are certain and His Word sure. The very nature of God, for He cannot lie, attests to the Truth that God has, does and will keep His promises, because it is impossible for Him to fail (Num. 23:19; Tit. 1:2).

Love (ágapaō). Love God. God is Love as to *His nature* (I John 4:8). It is the divine, self-sacrificing love, which is shed abroad in our heart by the Holy Spirit (Rom. 5:5). This love was manifested at the Cross. R. G. Lee stated, "The love of God was old when pyramids were new."

This Love is reciprocal, calling for obedience to our Lord, Who has saved us by His grace so that we might love and serve Him daily (Eph. 2:8—10; II Tim. 1:9).

TRANSLATION.

"Listen, my Brethren! Didn't God choose out for Himself the poor with reference to the world, Rich in Faith and heirs of the Kingdom which He promised to those who Love Him"?

James 2:6

"But you have despised the poor. Do not rich men oppress you, and draw you out before the judgment seats?"

But you (humeĩs dè). Despised (étímasate). Insult. It means to treat contumely: in word, deed or thought. *The Poor (tòn ptōchon).* One who is reduced to the situation of beggary, destitute of wealth, honor and position.

The object James has in view is quite plain. The poor visitor at the services, is far more likely to become a believer than the rich one. Believers, however, were treating the poor with churlishness, and giving exalted honor to the rich. The admonition was to treat both with the same kindness and friendliness.

James said, "You dishonored the poor and acted as if your Christian Faith had taught you. Whereas, it taught you the opposite." Look at your own numbers! How many of you would be heirs of the Kingdom if God would act as you do"?

The rich. They were the rich Jews who for the most part were Sadducees, named after Zadox, a priest who started them (II Sam. 8:17), at this period (A.D. 36—65), harassing poor Jews and Christian Jews.

Not (oúch). The word is used with a rhetorical question and expects the answer, "Yes." *Rich men (ploúsios). Wealthy.* "Those who are abounding in material resources." *Oppress (katadunasteúō). Harsh control over one. De*vilish (Acts 10:38).

There are "Examples in the papyri of harsh treatment by men in authority." "Poor Christians are feeling pressure from rich Jews as overlords." *You (humōn).* Rich Jews.

They were the unprincipled enemies of God, culprits, conducting themselves in wickedness as though nursed on tiger-milk cruelty, troubling Christians.

(áutoi) Reflexive, plural pronoun used emphatically: They themselves were guilty. *Draw (helkō). Drag off forcefully against* one's will. The word implies violence (Luke 12:58; Acts 8:3). *You (humās).* Believers were being troubled.

*Before (eís). I*nto. Judgments were handled in the law courts. "The words may indicate either to persecutions, or oppressive law-suits—perhaps both."

TRANSLATION.

"As for you, you dishonored the poor beggarly man. Do not men oppress you and draw you before the judgment seats"?

James 2:7.

"Do not they blaspheme that worthy name by which you are called"?

Blaspheme (blasphēmeō). Rail on one. Revile.

Worthy (kalón). Honorable. Noble. Excellent. Name (ōnoma).

Called (epíkaleō). The name which the Lord put upon His people, is *(Christian)* (Acts 11:26). *(Chrıstıanós). Follower of Christ,* saved by grace, redeemed by the blood of the Lord Jesus and has eternal life (Eph. 2:5; Heb. 9:22; I Pet. 1:18—20).

TRANSLATION.

"Do not they themselves speak reproachfully of the noble name (Christian) which was put upon you."

James 2:8.

"If you fulfill the royal law according to the scriptures, you shall love your neighbor as yourself, you do well- *If (ei). Assumed true. Fulfill (teleō). To bring to a close, finish. Royal (basilikon). Worthy of a king.* Ours is a *"Royal priesthood"* (I Pet. 2:9).

Metaphorically, the meaning is principal, chief. Loving God and loving one's neighbor, is the fulfillment "Of all the law and the prophets" (Matt. 22:37—40). The "Royal Law" was violated by partiality (*vs.* 2:3). The Christian must always treat the rich and the poor alike, showing partiality to neither.

Moody said, "One ransom price for all. So one in Christ, for all. Both within reach of rich and poor, who are on a level as regards redemption."

TRANSLATION.

"If you really fulfill the Royal Law according to the Scripture, you shall love your neighbor as yourself, you are doing excellently."

James 2:9.

"But if you have respect to persons, You commit sin, and are convinced of the law as transgressors."

Respect of persons (prosōpolēmpteō). Receive one's face. You commit sin (hamartía). Sin is missing the mark of God's glory (Rom. 3:23). *Commit (érgazomai).* Sin is the work of the Devil, using us in his program against God (Gen. 3:1, 4; Heb. 2:14).

Convinced (élegohō). Convict. Guilt. It refers to a rebuke which produces a conviction of the error of sin (John 3:20; 8:9).

Of the Law (*húpō*). *By. Agency.* The Law with the article, points to the previous reference, for the Law forbids, treating one, one way, another in an opposite way (James 2:8).

Transgressor (*parabainō*). *Step to one's side. Across.* Transgression is the passing beyond some assigned limit. It is breaking of a distinctly recognized commandment (Rom. 2:23; Heb.2:2; 9:15). Partiality is condemned (Lev. 19:15).

TRANSLATION.

"But if, assuming that, you are showing partiality (to the wealthy),
you are committing sin, being convicted by the Law as transgressors.

James 2:10.

"For whosoever shall keep the whole law, and yet offend in one *point,* he is guilty of all."

Shall keep (*tereō*). *Observe. Law* (*nómos*). Collectively. All Commandments. *Offend* (*ptaiō*). *Become.* Perfect tense shows a completed action in time past, having present results.

Guilty (*énechō*). It is to be guilty of anything. A lawbreaker has to stumble only one time. The Talmudic parallel: "If a man do all but omit one, he is guilty of each and all." This is a pertinent principle also for those who hope to save themselves. James is urging obedience to all God's Laws.

TRANSLATION.

"For whosoever shall keep the whole Law, but shall stumble in
one single (point), he is guilty of breaking all of it."

James 2:11.

"For he that said, Do not commit adultery, said also, Do not kill. Now, if you commit no adultery, yet if you kill, you are become a transgressor of the law."

Adultery (moicháomaı). *Sex with another man's wife.* Fornication is illicit sex in general (Matt. 19:9). Said (legō). Substance spoken. Kill (mḕ phoneúō) Murder.

"The unity of the Law, lies in the Lawgiver Who spoke both prohibitions, 'not' (*mē*)." The a*orist* denotes the fact of the action in past time. Murder springs from anger (Matt. 5:21—26).

Different choices have been attached to these commandments. "It is likely they are alleged as the first, duty to our neighbor generally."

Since everyone has at one point or another, transgressed the Law and in that the Law wasn't given to save us, we must not trust in its works, but in the Lord Jesus as Savior Who died at Calvary in our place. Jesus paid our sin-debt to God that we might be saved and have eternal life (Rom. 10:4; Gal. 2:20).

TRANSLATION.

"For He Who said, Do not commit adultery, also said, Do not kill. Now if, assuming that, you are not committing adultery but are committing murder, you have become a transgressor (of the) Law.

James 2:12.

"So speak you, and so do, as they that shall be judged by the law of liberty."

So (houtōs). In this manner. Speak you (laléō). The verbal action commands the doing and continuance of an act. The Christian is exhorted to comport himself always in a manner that his words, will bring glory to God.

"Let the words of my mouth, and the meditation of my heart be acceptable in your sight, O LORD, my strength, and my redeemer" (Ps. 19:14).

Do (poieìte). Perform. Doing follows speaking. Doctrine and deed go hand in hand. The believer will do well to substantiate his testimony with Christian conduct. The blessings of victorious living, are made possible through the Holy Spirit's enabling ministry.

Shall be judged (krínesthaınō). About to be judged. By (dìà). By means of. Law (nómos). Of Liberty. "The freedom of the law of Christ. It is the perfect Law, final and complete."

TRANSLATION.

"In such a manner be speaking and in such a manner, be habitually doing as those who are about to be judged by means of (the) Law of Liberty."

James 2:13.

"For he shall have judgment without mercy, that has shown no mercy; and mercy rejoices against judgment."

For (gàr). Reason (vs. 12 above). The Judgment (hē krísis). The article points to the coming judgment. *Without mercy (áneleōs).* Grace gives us what we don't deserve. Mercy is God withholding what we deserve.

Mercy (éleos). Pity. Those in distress. "Mercy is the principle of requital" (Matt. 5:7). *Boasts. (katakaucháomai). Triumph over.* "Only mercy can triumph over justice with God and man."

Chrysostom (347-407), golden mouth orator, stated, "Mercy is clothed with divine glory and stands by the throne of God."

TRANSLATION.

"For the judgment (will be) without mercy to him who did not show mercy; mercy triumphs over judgment."

James 2:14.

"What *does it* profit, my brethren, though a man may say he has faith, and have not works? Can faith save him?"

Profit (óphelos). Advantage. Brethren. A brother in Christ. Though (eàn). If (eàn). Hypothetical situation. A man (tis). Any one. Has (échō). Hold. Possession.

Faith (pístis). Faith in action. Trusting Christ for salvation (Acts 4:12). What about when there are no show of works? *Works (érga).* Works are the expected results of genuine faith.

Works are "Those acts in a believer's life are proofs and fruits of faith, not mere, ceremonial works." The dynamic of faith brings forth good works (Eph. 2:8—10; Tit. 3:8).

The words, "Can faith save him"? mean literally, that faith (without works just referred to) isn't able to save him, is it?" *Not (mē). Him (aútós).*

"As far as James is concerned, there is no question that true faith saves, but only true faith, and not a fruitless thing that one may call faith."

James isn't teaching the Galatian error to the effect that salvation is by faith, plus works, neither is he contradicting the Bible doctrine of justification by faith alone without works (Rom. 3:24—31; 4:4—22).

"James has exactly the same conception of saving faith Paul has when his Epistles declare, we are justified by faith without works of the law, a true and living trust in the Savior Jesus Christ.

"Paul doesn't have in mind one kind of faith when he says faith without works, saves, while James has in mind another kind of faith when he says without works, doesn't save. Both refer identically to the same kind of faith. Both attribute genuine faith to regeneration (James 1:18), justification and salvation."

Martin Luther called the Epistle of James an Epistle of straw and thought it contradicted justification in Romans.

Someone said to Spurgeon, "I hear you are opposed to works." "No," he said, "I am not, nor to chimney pots, but I would not put them at the foundation." As grace unfolds in a believer's life, there is salvation of the soul, followed by surrender and service (Rom. 6:16).

Moody, (the Professor of common sense), stated, "Faith justifies us in the sight of God. Works justify us in the sight of men. Faith without works is like a man putting all his money into a foundation of his house. Works without faith is like a man building without any foundation. A working faith is more than faith in works."

TRANSLATION.

"What is the profit, my brethren, if any one is saying that he has faith and has not works? That faith (without works) is not able to save him, is it?"

James 2:15.

"If a brother or sister be naked, and destitute of daily food."

If (eàn). Supposed. Brother (ádelphòs). Sister (ádelphē). Naked (gummoì). Clad in undergarment only, without sufficient clothing ((John 21:7). Destitute (leípō). Daily (émphēmeros). A day. Ephemeral. Food (trophē). Nourishment. Two common needs are mentioned: clothing and food.

TRANSLATION.

"But if a brother or sister has been without sufficient clothing for sometime and are lacking in daily food."

James 2:16.

"And one of you say unto them, Depart in peace, be *you* warmed and filled; notwithstanding, *you* give them not those things which are needful to the body, what *does it* profit?"

Depart (hupágete). Be going away. In Peace (eípēnēi). It is a common farewell among the Jews (I Sam. 1:17). The Lord Jesus used it (Mark 5:34; Luke 7:50). *Be warmed (thermaínō). Filled (chortázō) Satisfy with food.* Words only don't satisfy essential needs. Let us not be guilty of giving cold deeds with warms words (I John 3:18).

James "Takes an ordinary case of poverty to pinpoint an act of Christian faith and brotherly love, to give some help." Non is extended. Only words, "Goodbye, goodbye, be warmed and be fed—only I can do nothing for you! What do you think of a faith that produces such evidence?"

TRANSLATION.

"And one of (you) say to them, Be going away in peace, (be you) warming yourselves and be feeding yourselves; notwithstanding, but (you) do not give them the things needful to the body. What is the (profit)?"

James 2:17.

"Even so faith, if it has not works, is dead, being alone."

Even so (houtōs kai). In this manner. The Faith (hē pístis). With the article speaks of a previous reference to the faith of (*vs.* 14 above), which faith wasn't accompanied by good works.

Faith without good works, is dead. Salvation isn't merited or maintained by good works (Eph. 2:8-9). The believer practices good works because he is saved (Eph. 2:10). The proper place to put good works is right after salvation. Active faith results in good works.

If (eàn). Hypothetical case. Has (èchēi). He doesn't keep on bringing forth good works. *Works (èrga).* Works are the expected fruits of saving faith. Saving faith in the heart, produces good works in life. When one exercises God-given faith in the finished work of Christ, his soul is saved and there is a new relationship with God: good works follow.

Dead (nekrós). Being alone (éstín kath' heautēn). Robertson said, "In and of itself (*according to itself*), inwardly and outwardly, is dead—non-existent."

TRANSLATION.

"Thus, also the aforementioned faith, if it does not keep on constantly having works, is dead in itself."

James 2:18.

"Yea, a man may say, You have faith, and I have works: show me your faith without your works, and I will show you my faith by my works."

(Alla). But. A man (someone). Here is introduced "An imaginary objector who speaks one sentence: You have faith and I have works." There is an answer for the objector. James replies: "I have works also. Show me your faith apart from you works."

This one could be a member of the church who himself has no works; he is the *someone* of you mentioned in (2:16) who, for instance, puts off the naked and hungry with empty words." His faith was dead.

You (su). As for you, you have. Faith (pístis). Trust. Reliance. The objector is challenged to show his faith without works. "Show me a faith which is inconsistent with standing aloof, bidding the hungry, begone, feed himself, the naked clothe himself." Such faith is inconceivable. But I will show you my faith as evidence, proved by works of *mercy*.

Show (deíknumi). Give proof. The verb gives the command with military curtness and authority, to be obeyed at once. *Without (chōris). Apart from.* Works ought to accompany genuine faith. *I will show Exhibit.* The phrase, "By my works," is evidence of faith. Real, living faith in the soul, is outwardly demonstrated by good works.

TRANSLATION.

"But someone will say, as for you, you have faith and as for myself, I have works. Show me, at once, your faith apart from works, and I will show you my faith by my works.

James 2:19.

"You believe there is one God; you do well. The devils also believe and tremble."

You believe (pisteuō). Be persuaded of. Place confidence in. For emphasis: *As for you, you believe.* Keep on believing. *Is (éstin).* It is the ordinary verb of being, and often used to show the eternal being of our God (Heb. 11:6).

One God (heîs ho Theòs). There is focus upon the unity of the Godhead: Trinity: God the Father, and the Son and the Holy Spirit. One in essence, power and glory, a fundamental doctrine of the Christian Faith.

This truth proclaims each One in the Trinity and equal in adoration and worship. *You do well (kalōs poieîs). The devils (tà daimónia). Demons. There is only one Devil but many demons.* The demons never doubt the existence of God. Some today don't have as much faith as demons, for they scoff and make light of the Christian Faith.

Tremble (phrissō). Shudder. Bristle. The Christian trusts the Lord for salvation in confidence and faith, knowing his sins have been put away (Ps. 103:12).

The belief of the demons does nothing for them but certifies their own misery in heading for judgment. The Lord Jesus has authority and power over the demons.

The equality of the Godhead refutes Arianism and some other early heresies about the Deity and humanity of Christ

TRANSLATION.

"As for you, you believe there is one God. You are doing well. The demons also believe and shudder."

James 2:20.

"Will you know, O vain man, that faith without works is dead"?

Will you (thelō). Wish. Desire. It is the action of the will, governed by emotions. Deliberate action is (b*oúlomaı). Know (gınōskō). Knowledge. Based on experience. Oīda. Absolute knowledge* (I John 5:14). *Vain (kenós). Empty.* He is one "Void of knowledge, content with a dead and bootless notion."

Oīda points, "To the man whose head and heart should have been filled with the 'Word of truth' (1:18) and 'implanted Word'" (1:21). So that he might know what true faith is that no *someone* could come and persuade him to be satisfied with a faith no better than demons.

Man (ánthrōpos). That Faith (hē pístıs). The faith. (vvs. 14, 17-18 *above).* Without *(chōris). Apart from.* Works *(tōn érgōn). Fruits are evidence of faith. Inactive. Idle. Lazy.* Dead, *(nekrós),* is a non-working faith.

The fruitless person is like money which yields no interest, or like land uncultivated. It is barren (II Pet. 1:8). Lenski said, "The faith that is dead and barren, is only intellectual or a mere sentiment; it never attains anything substantial."

TRANSLATION.

"But do you wish to know, O empty man, that the aforementioned faith apart from works is inactive (barren, idle)?"

James 2:21.

"Was not Abraham, our father, justified by works, when he offered Isaac, his son, upon the altar?"

Abraham (*Abraàm). Father of multitudes* (Gen. 12:3). He is a type of the believer from the standpoint of faith (Gen. 15:6; Rom. 4:9, 11). Father: readers were Jews.

Spiritually, all believers in Christ, have a claim to the, title sons of or posterity of Abraham (Gal. 3:7, 29). The example of Abraham, proves that living faith is accompanied by works.

Justified (dıkaıóō). Vindicate. Justification here is before man; Paul speaks of justification before God (Rom. 3:24) as noted earlier by Moody. Justification is a man's vindication of his claim to have faith in the living Savior.

"Man looks on the outward appearance, but the Lord looks on the heart" (I Sam. 16:7). By works. Works of faith are *fruits of faith.*

He had offered (ánnénegkas). (Gen. 22:9—18; Heb. 11:17—19). His son (tón huiòn aútoũ). Upon (épi). On. The altar (tò thusiastērion). The altar of sacrifice.

TRANSLATION.

"Was not Abraham our father vindicated by works when he offered up his son, Isaac, on the altar of sacrifice

James 2:22.

"You see how faith wrought with his works, and by works was faith made perfect."

You see (blépō). Faith worked with the act of offering Issac on the altar of sacrifice. *His works (toĩs ẽrgais aútoũ). Outward proof of inward faith.*

By works (ék tōn ẽrgōn). Evidence of Abraham's, living faith. His faith (hē pístis). Abraham's. Perfect (ételeiōthē). Carry through completely. "The works were an exercise of faith."

TRANSLATION.

"You see that the aforementioned faith, was working with his works, and by works was his faith made complete."

James 2:23.

"And the scripture was fulfilled which saith, Abraham believed God, and it was imputed unto him for righteousness: and he was called the friend of God." *The* Scripture *(hē graphē). Was fulfilled (éplērōthē). Realization. Which saith (légō). Speak. Abraham believed (épísteusen dè) Persuaded. Trust. God (Theós).*

Genesis 15:6 proves the point in (*vs.* 2:21) that Abraham had works with his faith. He used the same verse Paul quoted in Romans 4:3, showing that Abraham's faith preceded his circumcision, and wasn't the basis of his justification. "James and Paul are right, each illustrating a different point."

Imputed (élogisthē). Put to one's account. Unto him (aútō). The dative case denotes being saved, is an individual matter, as it is the case of personal interest.

For (eis). Result of being saved. Righteousness (dikaiosúnē). Right standing before God. Justification (I Cor. 1:30). Friend of God (kaì Thoũ phílos). The Arabs speak of Abraham as a friend of God.

TRANSLATION.

"And the Scripture was realized in every particular which says, And Abraham believed God, and it was reckoned to him for righteousness, and a friend of God, he was called."

James 2:24.

"You see, then, that by works a man is justified, and not by faith only."

You see (hoāte). Discerning mind. "The conclusion is addressed to the brethren, no longer to the 'empty man.'" *(ánthrōpos kenós). Man (ánthrōpos). Representative man. That (hoti). By works. Out of (ek); Works (ĕrgōn). Fruits of faith. Is justified (dikaioũtai). Declared righteous.*

Not (oúk). Summary negation. Faith. Reliance. Trust). Only (mónos). "James is discussing the proof of faith, not the initial act of being set right with God" (Rom. 4:1—10).

"Live faith is what we must all have; only it must show itself in deeds as Abraham did." James isn't talking about the beginning of salvation, "But the way a saved person justifies his claim to a living faith in the Savior." Works are the proof of saving faith.

TRANSLATION.

"You see that by works a man is declared righteous, and not by faith only."

James 2:25.

"In like manner also was not Rahab, the harlot, justified by works, when she had received the messengers, and had sent *them* out another way?"

Rahab. Similar case. She was "Justified by works" in caring for the safety of the messengers who came to look over the land. *Not (oúk).* When used in a rhetorical question as here, expects the answer, "yes."

Was justified (ĕdıkaıōthē). Rahab's actions proved her faith. As with Abraham in *(vs.* 2:21). Rahab was "The wife of Salmon," ancestress of Boaz, Jesse's grandfather. Jesse was the father of King David.

Rahab was in the line of David and Christ (Matt. 1:1, 5-6). She is a hero of faith (Heb. 11:31). She left behind her sinful life-style, but the name clung to her always (Josh. 2:13).

God's grace reached Rahab's soul in redemption. The proffered mercy of God, avails for "The vilest of the vile," cleansing "The down and out," as well as, "The up and out." The Lord Jesus will save anyone who comes to Him (John 6:37).

By works. Out of (ĕk). Works (ĕrgōn). Outward fruits of faith. Rahab's faith was genuine and real, manifesting itself in living deeds for the glory of God (Matt. 5:16).

When she received (hupodexaménē). Welcomed. Receive as guests. The messengers were received secretly. *The messengers (toùs àggélous). Original meaning: Angels (*Matt. 11:10).

*Had sent them out (ĕkβalousa). Eager action. At once. Haste. Fear. Another way (heterai hodōi). Through a window (*Josh. 2:15).

Robertson stated, "So young was this woman's faith because it was genuine faith, it had corresponding works. She received the messengers, protected them and hurried them off."

TRANSLATION.

> *"And in like manner, also was not Rahab, the harlot, vindicated by works in that she secretly received as guests the messengers and thrust them by means of another way?*

James 2:26.

"For as the body is dead, so faith without works is dead also."

For (gàr). The body (tò sōma). The body—through which we have world-consciousness by means of the five senses: see, hear, smell, taste, touch. *Without (chōris). Apart from. Spirit (Pneúmatos). God- consciousness* (Prov. 20:17). When regenerated, man worships God "In Spirit and Truth" (John 4:24).

The body, without the spirit, is dead. *Faith (hē pístıs). The faith. Without (chōrìs). Apart from. Dead (nekrós).*

One writer commented, "It isn't easy to tell when one is dead, but the absence of a sign of breath on a glass before the mouth and nose, is proof of death. The words are a startling picture of dead faith in our churches, and church members with only a name to live" (Rev. 3:2).

This comparison has been found of surprise to some commentators, inasmuch as the things compared don't seem relatively to correspond. Faith is, without question, spiritual. Works equal obedience.

Many years ago a group of physicians in Kansas City, Missouri, examined a corpse, looking for a soul and spirit. Their report concluded man is without them. Walter Wilson, a Christian physician in K.C., offered this advice: "Next time man's soul and spirit are sought, don't look in an empty house."

TRANSLATION.

"For just as the body apart from the spirit is dead, so also faith apart from works, is dead (also)."

The Epistle Of James
Chapter Three

James 3:1.

"My brethren, be not many masters, knowing that we shall receive the greater condemnation."

My (mou). Brethren (ȧdélphoi). A Fellow-believer who is joined to fellow-believers. *Be (gínomaı). Become. Not (mē).* With the present imperative, there is a command to stop an action already in progress, stop becoming!

Masters (dídaskaloı). Teachers. A teacher is one who causes another to learn. He imparts knowledge to the congregation. The use is with a reference to the exhortation, S*low to speak (vs.2:19).* It is slow to begin speaking. Initial silence may stem garrulousness.

One author said, "Too many of the Jewish Christians, were attempting to teach what they didn't comprehend."

Teachers are necessary, but incompetent, unworthy, do much harm (I Cor. 14:26—34). A teacher has the greater responsibility."

K*nowing (eìdòtes). Beyond doubt.* The word is joined to the imperative: knowing as you do, or as you ought to know. *Greater (meīzon). Judgment (kríma). Condemnation. Sentence.* There is "A warning against the too eager and general assumption of the privilege of teaching."

Translation.

"Stop becoming many teachers, my brethren, knowing positively that we shall receive the greater sentence of judgment.

James 3:2.

"For in many things we offend all. If any man offend not in word, he *is* a perfect man, *and* able also to bridle the whole body."

For often (pollà gàr). We stumble *(ptaíomen). Trip. Stumble. All (âpsantes); (hapsantres). If anyone in word stumble not (eĩ tıs én lógōı ou ptaíomen). This one (oûtos);* (is); *a perfect (téleıos). (Full grown, mature Man (ánēr,* the individual man, not generic *(ánthrōpos).* Christian man.

Able (dunatòs). Powerful. Strong. To bridle (chalınagōgēsaı). Hold in check. Restrain. *Also the whole body (kaì ólon tó sōma).* "The Teacher uses his tongue constantly and so is in particular peril on this score."

The man who bridles his tongue, doesn't stumble in speech and able also to control his own body with all its passions. The tongue responds to sin most easily (*vs.* 1:26).

The control of the tongue is an important challenge to each Christian and every teacher of the gospel. God will look more closely at all teachers when He judges them. Teachers undertake to convey God's Word in the way in which God wants it conveyed, God will judge them .

TRANSLATION.

"For with reference to many things, we all stumble. If any anyone does not stumble in word (speech), this one is a mature, Christian man, able to restrain also the whole body."

James 3:3.

"Behold, we put bits in the horses' mouths, that they may obey us; and we turn about their whole body."

Behold, Idoú. Lo. Now if, such being the case. We put bits in the horses' mouths. The horses (tōn íppōn). The Hippōn. Genitive case. Behold! occupies an emphatic place in the sentence, showing the power and peril of the tongue. The tongue is a sharp sword (Ps. 57:4).

In the mouths (eís tà stómata). May obey (peithō). Yield. Comply. They may be obeying us. Turn *about (metagō).*

Seeing that horses may be brought into control by a small bit, should encourage believers to work on restraining the tongue for the glory of God in the blessing of the Holy Spirit.

"A soft answer turns away wrath, but grievous words stir up anger. The tongue of the wise uses knowledge aright, but the mouth of fools pours out foolishness" (Prov. 15:1-2).

It's in that moment of anger, irreparable harm may vent its malevolence in the cleavage of relationships as a nefarious spirit, strikes.

TRANSLATION.

"Now if, such being the case, we put bridles in the mouth of horses in order that they may be obeying us, also we turn about (guide) their whole body."

James 3:4.

"Behold also the ships, which, though *they be so* great, and *are* driven *by* fierce winds, yet are they turned about with a very small helm, wheresoever the governor lists."

Behold (Ἰδού). Demonstrative particle. "It gives a vivacity to the style by bidding the reader or hearer to attend to what is being said, "Behold! See! Lo!" *The ships (τὰ πλοῖα).* A more striking illustration since "Ships are larger than horses."

So great (τηλικαῦτα). Size (Rev. 16:18). The ship which took Paul to Malta, carried 276 passengers (Acts 27:37). *Fierce (σκληρῶν). Rough. Violent. Winds (ἀνέμω).*

Are turned about (metagō, vs. 3 above). With (hupò). Agency. Helm (pēdalion). Wheel. Rudder. "If James had only seen the modern, mammoth ships, like those anchored at Naval Ports."

Lists (βούλεται). Wills. Pilot. Charioteer. "Today it would apply to a chauffeur," one who leads or guides. Believers need to harness the tongue for salutary relationships.

TRANSLATION.

"Behold, also the ships, though they are so great and are driven by violent winds, are turned about by a very small rudder wherever the impulse of the steersman, deliberately wills."

James 3:5.

"Even so the tongue is a little member, and boasts great things. Behold, how great a matter a little fire kindles."

Even so (hutōs kaì). Thus. Also. A little member (mikrón mélos). Melos "Is an old and common word for members of the body" (I Cor. 12:12). *The tongue (glōssa).* A word is the smallest unit of speech when taken by itself, that has meaning.

Though a small member, the tongue causes great trouble with others along the path of life. Once spoken, words cannot be recalled.

And boasts great things (kaì megalaucheī). Lift up the neck. It is the posture of one who looks down his nose at others in prideful disdain.

It is shameless braggadocio, arrogant pretension. "There is no thought of an unfounded boast. The achievements on which the tongue prides itself, are real achievements."

"The tongue, though a small member like the little bridle and rudder, has gigantic capacity for either good or evil." "Neither filthiness, nor foolish talking, nor jesting which are not convenient; but, rather the giving of thanks" (Eph. 5:4).

Foolish talking (mōrología). Jesting (eùcharıstía).To turn (trépō). "Nimbleness of wit, quickness in making repartee, but in low sense as here ribaldry, scurrility, and wielding a wide range, is divisional."

The tongue causes disruption of effective communication. "In the multitude of words there lacks not sin, but he that refrains his lips, is wise" (Prov. 10:19).

Behold (ìdoú). How great (hēlıkon). Matter (hulēn). Forest. Little (hēlıkēn). Fire (pūr). Kindle (ànáptō). The tongue is a little spark. Forest fires were common in ancient times as now, usually caused by a small spark, carelessly thrown. A match can cause great destruction.

TRANSLATION.

"Thus, also the tongue is a small member and boasts great things. Behold, how great a forest a little fire sets aflame."

James 3:6.

"And the tongue is a fire, a world of iniquity; so is the tongue among our members that it defiles the whole body, and sets on fire the course of nature, and it is set on fire of hell."

This metaphor of fire is applied to the tongue (Proverbs 16:27; 26:18—22). "An ungodly man digs up evil, and in his lips there is as a burning fire." "Where no wood *is, there* the fire goes out; *so* where *there is* no talebearer, the strife ceases" (Prov. 26:20).

The World (ho kósmos). Iniquity (àdekías). The tongue is blighted by unrighteousness. Words may lift up or cast down. Words may cause healing or wounds. Words may encourage the distressed, rouse the careless, stir men and women to noble action with manifold blessings

Think of great orators like Cicero, (106-43 B.C.), who gave expression to the deeper emotions of life in the dynamic delivery of helpful words. A controlled tongue will brings forth words of delight, focus and joy.

The tongue is the embodiment of all wrong. It utters every wrong emotion, thought and puts every kind of wrong deed into words. "A wicked doer gives heed to false lips; *and* a liar gives ear to a naughty *destructive* tongue" (Prov. 17:4).

So (houtōs). In this manner (kathístatai). Genitive of possession. Members (mélē); (Rom. 12:4). *Defiles (spiloūsa). Spot (spilō).* "The tongue can play havoc in the members of the body; it pollutes the entire personality." Rumor is the art of saying nothing, while leaving nothing unsaid.

Sets on fire (phlogízō). Ignite. The course (tòn trochōn). Of nature (tēs genéseōs). Existence. (Wheel). The function was to revolve in a circle. Revolving continually on the same axis, was a common symbol among the Ancients, both for the changeableness and whole course of human existence.

Each life rolls onward from birth to death. There are many phrases and stages to complete the allotted cycle. Influence of the tongue, spreads out from the axle to the entire circumference of the wheel at every moment on its revolving course.

O! See what vicious propaganda does in a whole nation or in many nations. International hatreds are fanned into war. We must scuttle ill-will in relationships.

Consider the moral and spiritual field. "The teaching of popular religious and doctrinal errors, rages like vast conflagrations and leaves many victims in its wake." The whole round of existence is set aflame by a loose tongue.

Is set on fire of hell. (phlogizoménē). Present, passive of *(phlogízō),* speaks of continual source of the fire in the tongue. *Of (hupò). By. Hell. Gehenna.*

Another term for *Hell* is *(Haidēi),* now, temporary abode of the unsaved dead. The righteous dead were delivered from *(Haidēi)* at the resurrection of the Lord Jesus (Eph. 4:9-10).

The equal in the Old Testament, is *Sheol. Sheol/Haidēi* had two parts: one for the righteous and the other for the wicked dead (Luke 16:23).

Sheol was commonly referred to as Abraham's bosom (Luke 16:22). *Paradise* is the final resting place for the saved. Paul was caught up into Paradise, the third Heaven, the Throne of God. The word *unlawful* means *impossible to utter* (See II Cor. 12:4).

The wicked dead will be judged at the Great, White, Throne Judgment (Rev.20:11). Here in the context of James 3:6, *Hell, (Gehenna),* final abode of the wicked dead, called the *Lake of fire* (Rev. 20:14-15)

The worst description of the tongue shows that it is like the fire of *Gehenna. Gehenna,* the vale of Hinnōm, has the connotation of both defilement and fire. South of the walls of Jerusalem, lay the valley that had been desecrated by the worship of Molech, where children were burned (II Chron. 28:3; Jer. 7:31).

Josiah declared the place unclean. It was used as an offal dump. "And he defiled Topheth, which *is* in the valley of the children of Hinnom, that no man might make his son or daughter to pass through the fire to Molech" (II Kings 23:10).

There are two kinds of fire. There is a fire which purifies and illuminates, kindled in the soul by the Holy Spirit Who came down from above (Acts 2:2,3).

There is a fire that inflamed human emotions and infects life in its whole existence, kindled by the Devil, from beneath. It is the fire of *Gehenna,* awaiting the unrepentant sinner in judgment (Matt. 5:22; 18:9). Act now! "Today is the day of salvation" (II Cor. 6:2).

TRANSLATION.

"And the tongue is a fire, a world of iniquity: so is the tongue among our members , that it defiles the whole body, and sets on fire the course of nature; and is set on fire of hell."

James 3:7.

"For every kind of beasts, and of birds, and of serpents, and of things in the sea, is tamed, and has been tamed of mankind."

For (gàr). Fact. Kind (phúsis). Nature. It marks the relation between individual men and beasts, which may be different in different beasts. *Beasts (thērion). From (thēr).* At first, the reference was little beasts, then, wild animals in general or quadrupeds as here, beasts of the earth.

Of Birds (peteinōn). Flying animal. Fly (pétomai). Serpents (herpetōn). Creeping things. (1) *And of things in the sea (énalion).* Creation is fourfold in classification: (2) *quadrupeds (thēria);* (3) *birds (peteinōn);* (4) *reptiles (herpeta); to crawl (herpō).*

Is tamed (damázetai). Restrain. The present tense makes clear that such taming is not only a past fact but also a present reality in the history of the world. Man's lordship over the animals was established in the beginning (Gen. 1:28). *Mankind (ánthrōpinēi). Nature.* Beasts have been tamed by the skillful nature of man. At the original creation, God gave man "Dominion over the fish of the sea, and over the fowls of the air, and over every living thing that moves upon the earth" (Gen. 9:2).

All types of creatures, though not all of any one type, can, it would seem, may have actually been tamed by men. The strength of wild beasts, the fishes which inhabit a different element, the birds which are so quick in their flight—all subdued!

The serpents, with their death-bringing poison, have all alike succumbed to man. A Ranch, Zoo or Sea World, will fortify man's dominion.

Consider, Samson's phenomenal feat in catching 300 foxes and tying their tails together. He finished the project by putting a lighted torch between tails. The Philistines suffered great loss in their grain fields (Jud. 15:4). Samson also slew a young lion and honey, therein. Honey was a bonus (Jud. 14:5, 8).

Because of the Fall, man has lost dominion over himself. Born in the depravity and ruin of sin, man's only hope is in the finished salvation of God provided at Calvary, when the Lord Jesus died in our place (John 19:30; I Pet. 2:24).

Salvation is now available to all who will trust Christ (Acts 16:30-31; II Cor 6:2). Being saved, the believer will do well in yielding his life to the Holy Spirit for enabling grace to live the Christian life, pleasing to the Lord (II Cor. 12:9).

TRANSLATION.

"For every nature of beasts (quadrupeds) and birds and reptiles and marine life, is tamed and has been tamed by the nature of man."

James 3:8.

"But the tongue can no man tame; *it is* an unruly evil, full of deadly poison."

The tongue is a destructive, restless evil, ever a challenge to man to be controlled. Many times the tongue bruises, blights instead of blessing.

The tongue is like the death-dealing tongue of the asp before it strikes its mortal wound. The tongue has the potential to slays all in ramification of relationships.

No man (oúdeìs). Robertson stated, "Especially, his own tongue and by himself, but the believer has the help of the Holy Spirit in the challenge of harnessing the tongue" (Rom. 6:16). *Poison (ioū). Rust (vs. 5:3).*

The tongue is unstable and unlike the beasts, birds, fishes, serpents, man needs the help of the Lord in taming it. It is never fully, at rest, until brought under control.

TRANSLATION.

"But the tongue no one of men has power to tame. (it is) a restless evil, full of death-dealing poison."

James 3:9.

"Therewith bless we God, even the Father; and therewith curse we men, who are made after the similitude of God."

Therewith (én aùtēi). By means of. For (én) With Instrumental, case of means. Bless *(eùlogoūmen).* Good Word. Praises.

The highest expression of speech, is for the redeemed child of God to praise the Lord for his salvation (Jonah 2:9), reaching up to the highest mountain of eulogy, refreshing the soul at the fountain of living waters.

God (Kuríos). Lord. Father (Patéra). Provider, Protector, Upholder. He also nourishes us, meeting our daily need (Phil. 4:19). The omnipotent Lord of Heaven and earth, is our Father through our redemption in Christ Jesus (John 1:12-13; 3:16-17).

While God is the Creator of all men, He is the Father only of believers (I Thess. 3:11, 13). It is a blessed truth we are drawn to fellow-believers by the bond of grace into a heavenly brotherhood.

The Epistle is addressed to Christians (Jas. 1:1); *Love (ágápē).* It is possible for a believer only to manifest this love which is shed abroad in the believer's heart by the Holy Spirit" (Rom. 5:5).

*Hope, (élpís), (*Rom. 5:5), denotes one assured of his salvation in Christ. *Fellow-believers* are joined to the Savior and to one another by salvation which is anchored in Christ (Heb. 6:19).

Curse (katàra). Imprecate evil. Men are the objects of wicked tirades of the tongue set on fire by Hell. The magnitude of the sin of hurling, fiery curses upon men, is shown by the words, "Which are made after the similitude of God."

Made (gegonótas). Created. The truth is that men still have upon them the marks of their divine origin. *After (kath'). In. Similitude (homoíōsın). Likeness. Image.* (Gen. 1:26). *God (Theoū).* Genitive of description—*God's image.*

Man, through deliberate rebellion against his benign Creator, fell into the total ruin of sin. However, He still has the image of God in him, though that image is marred by sin. It is this image of God, which sets man above the beasts (II Cor. 3:18). "For one to curse man is, in effect, to curse God Himself"

Each man has an immortal spirit with a will, knowledge, self-consciousness. Those personality qualities have been injured by the Fall, but not destroyed.

The point of this reference to the likeness of God, is the close relationship between God and man. This brings to light the enormity of what the tongue does, in blessing one and cursing the other, to think it can do both.

The fact, relating to the image of God in man now, doesn't in any way mean that one can save himself by goods works, for man hasn't, in himself, anything to merit the favor of God's salvation.

Man is totally dependent upon the grace of God for the salvation of the soul (Rom. 4:4-5). Salvation is received by grace, when one trusts Christ as personal Savior (Acts 4:12).

Our "Righteous deeds are as filthy rags" (Isa. 64:6; Tit. 3:5). The restlessness of the tongue is exemplified by its inconsistency in blessing God and cursing man.

TRANSLATION.

"By means of it (the tongue), we bless the Lord, even the Father, and by means of it, we curse (imprecate evil on) men who have been made in the image of God."

James 3:10.

"Out of the same mouth proceeds blessing and cursing. My brethren, these things ought not so to be."

Out of (ék). Mouth (stómatos). Proceeds (éxérchetai). Goes forth. Blessing (eúlogía). Cursing (katápa). My brethren (ádelphoí mou). In Christ.

These things (taūta). The meaning shows the inconsistency of the tongue in giving blessing and pronouncing cursing. *Ought not to be (oútōs); (houtōs). No (oúdemía). It isn't right. Fitting.*

Ryrie commented, "The point is that a believer's tongue should not speak inconsistencies." It is a striking, moral incongruity for blessing and cursing to come out of the same mouth. There is some repetition here. However, repetition is the Mother of learning.

So (houtōs). In this manner. To be (gínomai). Become. Continuous action. These things ought not to keep on taking place. The tongue vents a lot of heartache.

TRANSLATION.

> *"Out of the same mouth comes forth blessing and cursing. My brethren, these things ought not thus, to keep on constantly taking place."*

James 3:11.

"Does a fountain send forth at the same place sweet water and bitter"?

*Fountain (pēgē). Spring (*John 4:14). *Send forth (bruō). Bubble. Gush forth.* It is an expressive word and speaks of a full, copious discharge, as budding plants. *Opening (ópēs). Hole* or *Rock* in the earth. *Sweet water* and *bitter. Sweet (glukù). Bitter (píkrón).* "There is no need to supply anything: the contrast is in the opposite nature of the two."

Two articles are used to distinguish sharply each. The inconsistency of blessing and cursing with the same mouth, is as unnatural as for a fountain to gush forth sweet and bitter water simultaneously, out of the same mouth.

Common, natural things which don't mix, are used to drive home the point of harnessing the tongue to bring blessing instead of cursing.

TRANSLATION.

"The spring out of the same opening, does not gush forth the sweet and the bitter."

James 3:12

"Can the fig tree, my brethren, bear olive berries? Either a vine, figs? So can no fountain yield both salt water and fresh."

Can (dúnatós). Able. Strong. Have power. Make (poiéō). Produce. Fig tree (sūka). Olive berries (élaías). Again, persuasive words, in things, which do not mix. A law of nature shows like produces like—root—fruit.

There is no crossing over from one to the other. The Lord Jesus pointed out to His disciples that "Grapes are not gathered from thorn-bushes nor figs from thistles" (Matt. 7:16). *Salt (álukòn); (halukòn). Fresh (glukù). Sweet.*

TRANSLATION.

"A fig tree, my brethren, does not have power to produce olives, does it, or a vine, figs? Neither does salt water have power to produce sweet water."

James 3:13.

"Who is a wise man and endued with knowledge among *you?* Let him show out of a good conversion his works with meekness of wisdom."

Wise (sophòs). It is the word used for the practical teacher of (*vs.* 3:1). True wisdom comes from God. Wisdom has two parts: (As God sees it; as man sees it). *Knowledge (genōsıs). Wisdom (sōphías). Understanding (epıstēmōn). Good judgment.*

Knowledge gathers facts. *Wisdom* is the best use of facts in making wise decisions that honor and please the Lord. *Understanding* will manifest itself in prudent behavior. Solomon prayed for all three in leading and guiding God's so great a people (II Chron. 1:10-11).

Endued with knowledge (epıstēmō). He is an expert, a skilled, scientific person with a tone of superiority. (*Sophòs*). It is broader, more general; perhaps, more dignified term of the two.

Wisdom (sophós). Special, intelligent application, exercised for the quality of particular things. (épıstēmōn). Able individual (sophós). Well-informed ı The right use of wisdom and knowledge, are contrasted with perverted evil.

Let him show (deíxátō). *Exhibit Meekness (én praíûtētı). Wisdom (sophías). (vs.* 1:21). Now, comes the time for Christians to show on the outside that salvation in the soul.

The pattern will be to put belief into behavior: creed into conduct doctrine into deeds. It is justification before men—the theme of James. The call goes forth to each individual in this demonstration of living the Christian life.

TRANSLATION.

"Who is wise and understanding among you? Let him exhibit out a good (and excellent) manner of life his works in meekness and true wisdom."

James 3:14.

"But if you have bitter envying and strife in your hearts glory not, and lie not against the truth."

If (ei). Assumed true. *Have* (ἔchete). You are having. Envying (zēlon). *Jealousy* (Rivalry).

Pride is in the mix here. Robertson commented, "Pride of knowledge is evil and leaves a bad taste (I Cor. 8:1). It's a slippery board to jealousy, which is 'As cruel (hard) as the gave'" (Song of Sol. 8:6).

Jealousy causes people to do strange things. Jealousy breeds hatred. Carver said, "He who hates will be destroyed by hatred." After the Civil War President Lincoln said, "Charity to all and hatred toward none."

Bitter envy (Party spirit). One who pushes forward for personal ends. The word came to be applied to those who serve in official positions, for their selfish interest who promoted division.

Strife (zēlon). *Disrupts harmony.* A call comes forth for: "One spirit, one accord, one mind" (Phil. 1:27; 2:2). "Behold, how good and how pleasant *it is* for brethren to dwell together in unity" (Ps. 133:1).

Your Heart (tēı kardíaı). Out of the heart proceed our thoughts, words, deeds.

God uses the heart to make things run smoothly. "The LORD looks on the heart" (I Sam. 16:7). The path to victory is to let the emotions of the heart reign.

*Glory (katakauchāsthe). Glory against. Not (*mē). It boosts one's self to the injury of another. It is a tirade of disrespect. The full meaning of *glory not* is, "Stop constantly boasting."

"Be you kind one to another, tenderhearted forgiving one another, even as God, for Christ's sake, has forgiven you" (Eph. 4:32). "In honor preferring one another" (Rom. 12:10). Then, the sweet waters of spiritual blessings will bring invigoration to all in the good hope of grace.

Lie (pseūdesth). Deceive. Speak deliberate falsehood. The Truth (tēs álētheias). "Lying against the Truth is futile. By your own conduct do not belie the Truth which you teach; solemn and needed lesson" (Rom. 1:18; 2:18, 20).

TRANSLATION.

"But if, such being the case, you are having bitter jealousy and (rivalry, faction and party spirit) in your heart, stop constantly boasting and lying against the Truth."

James 3:15.

"This wisdom descends not from above, but is earthly, sensual, devilish."

This Wisdom (hautē hē sophía). False wisdom. This wisdom; namely, the wisdom that is all talk and no action (*vss.* 1:5; 3:17). *Not (oúk). Negation. From above (ánōthen). But (àll'). Strong. Contrast.* "It is clear this wisdom isn't God-given, for the source is devilish."

This wisdom is bound by earthly limitations as in (Phil. 3:19). Man's wisdom is conditioned and limited at all points by his unregenerate mind, apart from the Holy Spirit.

Natural man (psuchikē ánthrōpos). "But the natural man receives not the things of the Spirit of God; for they are foolishness unto him, neither can he know *them* because they are spiritually discerned *(understood)*" (I Cor. 2:14).

Earthly (epígeios). "Man's wisdom has its origin to earth-bound motives, even when heavenly things are looked into." *Sensual (psuchikē). Non-spiritual.* The word refers to the gratification of the senses or appetite. Some see it as jungle-like behavior. The natural man is far from God in thought and life-style.

Devilish (*daimoniōdēs*). *Diabolical.* There is one Devil but many demons. It is demon-like, not God-like (I Tim. 4:1). The Devil influences men to reject God's proffered grace (Eph. 2:2). "The fool has said in his heart, *There is* no God..." (Ps. 14:1).

Fool is like a branch cut off, detached from the life of the tree. This wisdom doesn't come down from above, but is earthly, sensual, demon-like.

TRANSLATION.

"This wisdom is not one coming down from above, but is earthly, sensual, (non-spiritual), demon-like."

James 3:16.

"For where envying and strife *are*, there is confusion and every evil work."

For (gàr). Where (ópou); (hopou). Jealousy (zēlos). Strife (éritheía). Rivalry. Coping. Confusion (àkatastasía). Instability. Restlessness.

Every (pán). Every kind. Evil (phaūlon). Worthless. Thing; Work (prāgma). God put man to work even before the Fall (Gen. 2:15). Activity is good for man's well-being. Good works are a testimony (Tit. 2:14).

TRANSLATION.

"For where jealousy and rivalry exist, there is restlessness (and) every kind of base (wicked, bad deed).

James 3:17.

"But the wisdom that is from above *is* first pure, then peaceable, gentle *and* easy to be entreated, full of mercy and good fruits, without partiality, and without hypocrisy."

But the (hē dè). Wisdom (sophía). From above (ánōthen). It comes down from God's dwelling place in Heaven. *First (prōton). Inner quality. Pure (ágnē); (hagnē).* It is pure in itself, wholly free from any defilement.

We are edified in the assurance of God's wisdom. *Then peaceable (eírēnikē). Loving peace.* It never starts quarrels, strife, dissension or turbulence. "But clearly as peace is, purity: *(righteousness)* comes before peace."

Francis of Assisi, (1182-1226), prayed, "Lord, make me an instrument of peace." Peace lifts harmony to the highest plateau of concord and maturity. The peace of salvation comes when Christ is received as personal Savior (Rom. 5:1).

Gentle (épieikḗ). Equitable. (Phil. 4:5; I Pet. 2:18). The heavenly wisdom is considerate in demands made upon others. *Easy to be entreated (eúpeithēs). Complaint. Open to reason.* Docile and willing to submit to reasonable requests.

Full of mercy (mestè éléous). Compassion. Good fruits (karpōn). "Good deeds are the fruit of righteousness" (Phil. 1:11).

Without partiality (ádiákritos). Without hypocrisy (ánupókritos). This wisdom isn't a play actor, doesn't wear the hypocrite's mask. It is sincere, unfeigned (Rom. 12:9).

TRANSLATION.

"But the wisdom from above, is first (essentially) pure, then peaceable, reasonable, compliant, full of mercy and good fruits, impartial, free from hypocrisy (sincere)."

James 3:18.

"And the fruit of righteousness *is* sown in peace by them that make peace."

Righteousness (dikaiosúnē). Justification. "Being justified freely by his grace through the redemption that is in Christ Jesus" (Rom. 3:24). God saves us from death to deliverance, from sin to salvation and from ruin to redemption.

Salvation is all of God: from start to finish, from A to Z, from its inception on earth to its glorious consummation in Heaven (Jonah 2:9; Acts 13:39).

Salvation in the soul brings forth fruit in the life. There is "Fruit, more fruit, much fruit" (John 15:2- 5). There are hundred, sixty and thirty-fold fruit-bearers (Matt. 13:23). Be a hundred-fold, fruit-bearer.

Is sown (speírō). Scatter seed. "Only in peace is the fruit of righteousness found." *Peace (eírēnēn). Peacemakers, Sons of God* (Matt. 5:9). Pastor and people are mutually respectful. In loving one another, the Lord is honored (I Thess. 5:13).

TRANSLATION.

"And the fruit of righteousness is sown in peace for those making peace."

CHAPTER FOUR

James 4:1.

"From where *come* wars and fights among you? *Come they* not hence, *even* of your lusts that war in your members?"

From where (píthen). Inquire of the origin of *wars* and *fights. Wars (pólemai). Dispute. Quarrel.* Those words describe the chronic state and campaign. A church has a poor testimony in the community, when the people of God can't get along with each other.

Fights (máchai). A battle. There are separate conflicts in the war. *Among (én).* The word is used with the dative, case of personal interest. It speaks of association. *You (humīn). Jewish believers of the dispersion.* "So the forcing of wrath brings forth strife" (Prov. 30:33).

From within (*ék*). *Ablative case. Source of* quarrels. *Fights.* Lusts (*hēdonōn*). *Sinful, sensual pleasure. That war (tōn strateuoménō).* Robertson wrote, "It means to carry on a campaign, here as in (I Pet. 2:11), of the passions of the human body."

James seems to be addressing nominal Christians. Modern church disturbances are old enough in practice. "Yield yourselves *as* servants to obey," the Lord (Rom. 6:16).

TRANSLATION.

"From what source are quarrels and fights among you? Do they not come out of your sinful pleasures which are constantly campaigning in your members."

James 4:2.

"You lust, and have not; you kill, and desire to have, and cannot obtain; you fight and war, yet you have not, because you ask not."

You lust (épthumeīte). Yearn. Desire. The context decides its meaning: good or bad. Here it is used in an evil sense. *Have not (oùk échete). Do not possess.*

You kill (phonévete). Ryrie stated, "The logical, but not necessarily usual outcome of lust." Mayor said, "You murderously envy." *Desire to have (zēloō).* You boil with envy and anger.

Cannot obtain (oú dúvasthe épitucheīn). Sinful lusting will not receive anything from God. Ropes commented, "Make the service of God your supreme end, and then your desires will be such as God can fulfill in answer to your prayer" (Matt. 6:31-33; Ps. 84:11).

You Fight (máchesthe). Quarrel. War (pólemos). Dispute. You ask not (húmās mè aiteīsthe). "And whatsoever we ask, we receive of him because we keep his commandments, and do those things that are pleasing in his sight" (I John 3:22).

Rice said, "Prayer is the ordained means by which God supplies the needs of His children." "If you abide in me, and my words *abide* in you, you shall ask what you will, and it shall be done unto you" (John 15:7). *Abide (meínēte). Home.* Make Jesus Headquarters of your life.

TRANSLATION.

"You have a yearning desire for, and you do not possess; you kill. And you boil with envy and anger, and you are not able to obtain. You quarrel and fight. You have not because you are not praying for something to be given you."

James 4:3.

"*You* ask, and receive not, because you ask amiss, that you may consume *it* upon your lusts."

You ask (aiteīte). For something to be given. Receive not (lamβinō ou). Ask amiss (aiteisthai kakōs). Evilly. They prayed for selfish purposes.

That (hína). In order that. Consume it (dapanēstē). To spend. Waste. Squander. Your Lusts (taīs hēdonaīs). Sinful pleasures war against the soul to sidetrack one, seeking higher heights of fulfillment. Praying aright eliminates a craving for sinful enticements.

God's ears are opened to the cry of the righteous (Ps. 34:15); nigh to all that call upon Him in Truth (Ps. 145:18); prayers offered according to the will of God (I John 5:14). The prayers of all such ascend directly to the throne of grace (Heb. 4:16).

TRANSLATION.

"You pray for something to be given you and do not receive because you pray with evil intent for something to be given you in order that you may spend it in your sinful pleasures."

James 4:4.

"You adulterers and adulteresses, know you not that the friendship of the world is enmity with God? Whosoever, therefore, will be a friend of the world, is the enemy of God."

Adulterers (moichoi). Marriage is for keeps. When one steps out of that relationship and marries another, he becomes an adulterer (Matt. 19:6).

Adulteresses (moíchalídes). The same applies to the woman. However, there is one exception for breaking the marriage relationship: *Fornication* (Matt. 19:9). Too many marriage issues are taken to be *fornication;* obviously, there are other issues.

"Adulteresses is a stern but true verdict of the condition of the Epistle's recipients, showing their guilt and shameful deportment. This one scathing word is sufficient. It should produce deep contrition and prompt amendment." *Adulterers* and adulteresses are a designation for their friendship with the world. They have ignored the Lord.

Israel is represented as the wife or betrothed bride of God. Her unfaithfulness is recorded in these words, "They go a whoring from you" (Ps. 73:27; Ezek. Chap. 16). Likewise, the Church is called upon to be faithful to God (Rev. 2:4).

Know you not (oúk.oîdate). Know with positive assurance. It is used here, however, to "Express surprise and shock. They act as if they didn't even know."

The friendship (hē philía). Of the world (toû kósmos). The world refers to men and their interest. The world is without God, ungodly to the core. It is the world's evil system, headed up by Satan, polluted, corrupted religiously, socially and politically (Eph. 2:2; I John 5:19). Ryrie stated, "It's spiritual adultery," to love the world.

Enmity (échthòs). Enemy. With (toū). Of. God (Theoū). In redemption man is released from the world, so that he might triumphant over it in the power of the Holy Spirit. By right of redemption, one becomes a member of God's family (Eph. 3:14-15).

To walk in the ways of the world, one will enter eternity without God. God and the world stand opposite to each other. One cannot join one without deserting the other (Matt. 6:24; John 15:19). Satan continue to snare souls (Heb. 9:27).

Whosoever (ôs); (hos); (àn). Emphatic word. Therefore (oun). It draws a conclusion, connecting sentences logically. *Will (boulēthēi). Will deliberately. Minded.* One must be ever spiritually alert so as not to become a friend of the world, giving up his devotion to God.

TRANSLATION.

> *"O! You adulterers and adulteresses, do you not know with positive assurance that your friendship with the world, is enmity with God? Whoever, therefore, would purpose deliberately to be a friend of the world, establishes (himself) as an enemy of God."*

James 4:5.

"Or do you think that the scripture says in vain, The spirit that dwells in us lusts to envy"?

Or (ē). Think (dokeīe). Suppose. Subjective judgment. The Scripture (hē graphē). The Word of God is personified as in (*vs.* 2:23; Gal. 1:8). *Says (légei). To speak. In vain (kenós). Empty way. No purpose.*

The Spirit (the Holy Spirit). *Dwells (katōikēsen). Permanent residence.* The Holy Spirit has been caused to take up His permanent residence in our hearts.

What blessed, condescending grace the Holy Spirit has been caused by the Father to make His permanent home in us, in answer to our Savior's prayer (John 14:16).

The Holy Spirit indwells every believer from the moment of regeneration. He will never leave the believer, assuring each Christian of eternal life. The Holy Spirit enables the believer to live a life pleasing to God. Sin grieves Him. *Jealous envy (pròs phthónon épipotheī),* causing problems in the church.

TRANSLATION.

"Or, do you think that the Scripture speaks to no purpose, The (Holy) Spirit who has been caused to take up His permanent home in us, has an earnest desire (for complete sway over us) to (the degree of) jealous envy?"

James 4:6.

"But he gives more grace. Wherefore, he says God resists the proud, but gives more grace to the humble."

He gives (dídōsin). More grace (meízona. dè). Greater grace. Grace (chárın). Undeserved gift. There is a grace that saves, keeps us and gives us good hope for the future.

Hope (élpìs) (Rom. 5:5). *Assurance.* There are "The riches of his grace" (Eph. 1:7); "The exceeding riches of his grace" (Eph. 2:7); "The unsearchable riches (of grace)" (Eph. 3:8).

William Jennings wrote, "The amazing grace of God is that work of God whereby He does the unexpected for the undeserving, providing the unattainable, the reason non-explainable, the result undeniable, the benefit: unchangeable, unrepayable, unending."

"Grace is righteous salvation for those who deserve righteous condemnation." "Grace is a boon purchased by the court that found us guilty."

It is contradictory to surmise one may lose his salvation. The words, "You are fallen from grace," Presents a problem to many (Gal. 5:4). It is sanctifying grace. An Authority stated, "To use the impossible ground of justification by law, is to leave, abandon, fall from the way of grace as the only basis for justification."

Saved (Paraphrastic Present). Ephesians 2:8, "For by the grace you have been saved in the past completely, with the present result you are now in a state of salvation which persists through present time"

Wherefore (dìò). On which account. It is the strongest, inferential conjunction. *He* (the Holy Spirit) says, "God resists the proud." *God (Theòs). Resist (ántıtássetai). Range in battle against.* Middle voice: sets himself in array against.

The Proud ('hupēphánoıs). Show one's self. The picture is that of a man with his head held high above all others. The proud are consumed with position, power, prominence and self.

"Every one *that is* proud in heart *is* an abomination unto the LORD; *though* hand *join* in hand, he shall not be unpunished" (Prov. 16:5).

Grace (chárın). It is the enabling grace of God by the Holy Spirit, day-by-day, in walking with the Lord. *Humble (tapeınoîs).* "Those who recognize their insufficiency, are conscious of their, lowly, creature estate, absolute dependence upon Almighty God and are willing to receive from Him, and Him alone, all that is necessary for their salvation."

"Grace for grace" is "Grace on top of grace" (John 1:16). "The lowly or humble realize that they have nothing. They are happy to receive God's rich grace which satisfies their souls."

God's grace is like an artesian well, the demand of which never depletes the supply. Here is the proof that the ambitious and restless after worldly honors and riches, are the enemies of God.

But the humble and lowly are objects of His gifts of ever-increasing grace. "But where sin abounded, grace did super abound and some on top of that" (Rom. 5:20).

The humble recognize all they have, comes from God and others in his pilgrimage to the Father's house (John 14:1—6). Jesus said, "Blessed *are* the meek; for they shall inherit the earth" (Matt. 5:5).

TRANSLATION.

"Moreover, He, (the Holy Spirit), gives greater grace. On which account He (the Holy Spirit) says, God sets Himself in array against the proud and haughty, but gives grace to the humble and lowly."

James 4:7.

"Submit yourselves, therefore to God. Resist the devil, and he will flee from you."

('Hupotagēte). Place under. Obey. Be subject. It is to place one's self to be a servant. The aorist imperative is issued with military authority and demands, on-the-spot obedience with decisive finality. *To God (tōi Theōi).* God is worthy of our deepest trust and undivided worship.

The believer yields total obedience to the Lord—once for all (Rom. 12:1-2). We were the servants of sin. We are now the servants of God (Rom. 6:16). From dedication comes spiritual blessings, strength and daily victory.

Resist (ȧntístēte). Stand against. Oppose. The Devil (tōı dıabólōi). The s*landerer.* Created a mighty, angelic spirit, Lucifer (light bearer, shining one), "Son of the morning" (Isa. 14:12), "Anointed cherub" (Ezek. 28:14), who through willful sin against God, became the Devil, Satan, liar, murder (John 8:44).

The Devil is "The god of this world" (II Cor. 4:4), "The prince of the power of the air" (Eph. 2:2), tempter (I Thess. 3:5), accuser (Rev. 12:10). He is the personal, pernicious adversary. The Devil is the arch-enemy of God and man. *Will flee (pheúxetai). From you (aph' 'humōn).*

The Christian is called upon to withstand, resist and oppose the Devil in the power and strength of the Lord. There is spiritual triumph for the Christian who gives complete obedience to God.

"And they overcame him by the blood of the Lamb, and by the word of their testimony, and they loved not their lives unto the death" (Rev. 12:11).

TRANSLATION.

*"Accordingly, be obedient with complete subjection to God.
Stand against the Devil and he will flee away from you."*

James 4:8.

"Draw nigh to God, and he will draw nigh to you. Cleanse *your* hands, *you* sinners; and purify hearts, *you* double-minded."

Draw nigh (éggízō). Come near. It was used in the Septuagint of the priests entering the temple to offer sacrifices or to perform other ministrations (Lev. 10:30).

We draw nigh unto God, meaning to turn one's thoughts to God, to become more acquainted with Him (Heb. 7:19). It is a joyous journey for the Christian to walk in the sunlight of God's glory and grace.

He will draw (éggıeī). Come. Nigh to you ('humin). He isn't a God far off but near at hand. God is our Father through the redemptive salvation, we have in Christ (Rom. 3:24). The Lord is just a prayer away.

When the Christian chooses to come close to God, the Lord will come close to him. God the Father and the Lord Jesus, make their home in our hearts (John 14:23).

The right to come close to God and to know He is near, distinguishes God's people from the world. "Let us, therefore, come boldly, (*with freedom of speech*), to the throne of grace, that we obtain mercy and find grace in time of need" (Heb. 4:16).

NEAR TO GOD

"Nearer to God, I could not be,
For in His Son, I'm just
As near to God as He."
-Ironside

Israel was also very special to God. "For what nation *is there so* great, who *has* God so nigh unto them, as the LORD our God *is* in all things that we call upon Him *for?"* (Deut 4:7).

Under the Law, it was the special function of the priests to come near to God at set times to offer sacrifices on behalf of the people (Exod. 19:22).

Under Grace, the privilege is open to all believers any time. We come not with hands laden with sacrificial gifts. We plead only the shed blood of Jesus (I Pet. 1:19). *Cleanse (katharísate). Moral* cleansing, not *ceremonial (*Acts 21:24, 26).

Hands (cheíras). Hands are so involved in our actions and sometimes "blood stained" (Isa. 1:15). Hands focus on deeds (I John 3:18). "Clean hands; pure heart" (Ps. 24:4). *Sinners ('harmartólos). One devoted to sin.*

An authority commented, "Sinners! A sharp word to strike the conscience, a reproach meant to startle and sting." The word is often used of men guilty of a certain, definite sin—as David (II Sam. 11:1—5).

Cleanse ('hagnizō). The Christian's whole life is to be one of constant purification. *Hearts (kardías).* "The *heart* is the seat of the thoughts, will, inner source of all our actions."

"Trust in the LORD with all your heart, and lean not unto your own understanding. In all your ways acknowledge him, and he shall direct your paths. Be not wise in your own eyes; fear the LORD, and depart from evil"(Prov. 3:5-7).

Double-minded (dípsuchos). Double-souled That person's affections are split between God and the world. Being doubled-souled is an ungodly condition, spiritual weakness. The remedy is re-dedication of one's whole self to Christ and a fresh submission to the cleansing power of the Holy Spirit (Rom. 12:1-2).

"Let the words of my mouth, and the meditation of my heart, be acceptable in your sight, O LORD, *my* strength, and my redeemer" (Ps. 19:14).

TRANSLATION.

"Draw near to God, and He will draw near to you. Cleanse (your) hands, O sinners, and purify (your) hearts, O double-souled"

James 4:9.

"Be afflicted, and mourn, and weep; let your laughter be turned to mourning, and *your* joy to heaviness."

Be afflicted (talaipōrēsate). Feel miserable. Drawing near to God, involves heart-searching, for "The sacrifices of God *are* a broken spirit: a broken and a contrite heart, O God, you will not despise" (Ps. 51:17).

The believer must be deeply exercised in his soul over sins against God, resulting in the joy of living triumphantly.

Mourn (pénthos). Weep (klaiō). Weep audibly. To cry like a baby. There is "A call to godly sorrow" in (I Cor. 7:10). Mayor said, "Like an Old Testament prophet." Jeremiah was "The weeping prophet." The readers are "To feel miserable, mourn, and to cry aloud" over their past, worldly, sinful double-life.

Your ('humōn). Laughter (gelōs). Mirth. Joy. It isn't the true joy of God, but "Laughter born of flippancy, scorn and self-satisfaction." It was a false gaiety of sinful pleasures, compounded with a failure to realize sin's true nature.

Be turned (metastraphētō). Turn around. Grief. Sorrow. Mourning (pénthos). O! that revival fires would burn again across our land in our souls in these troubling times.

Your (hē) Article. Possessive pronoun. Joy (chará). Gladness. Heaviness (katēpheian). Casting down the eyes. Shame. Dejection. Gloom.

Only when they accepted the invitation to mourn and weep, would the blessedness of God's kingdom come on the wings of mercy. Then, holy, guileless laughter,will be seen in the company of the saints.

TRANSLATION.

"Be miserably afflicted, mourn and cry aloud. Let your laughter be turned to grief and your gladness to dejection."

James 4:10.

"Humble yourselves in the sight of the Lord, and he shall lift you up."

Humble yourselves (*tapeinōthēte*). Bring low. It means to confess and deplore one's littleness and unworthiness before the Lord. The humble are occupied with God's will and Word.

The humble person knows all he has in his life, is from God, and others who touch his life. Blessed, (spiritually prosperous). The Lord will guide the meek in justice and teach him His ways (Ps. 25:9).

In the sight (énōpion). In presence of. Lord (Kuriou). "God the Father" (*vs.* 1:7). In drawing near to God in humility, the believer is more aware of being in the presence of the Lord. In subjection to Him, the Christian recognizes His providence and justice.

He will lift ('hupsōsei). Lift up on high. Exalt. You ('humas). Believers. The Lord will exalt His people both here and hereafter. He performs that work now by His grace. In His time, He will bring forth His waiting children.

"Humble yourselves, therefore, under the mighty hand of God, that he may exalt you in due time" (I Pet. 5:6).

TRANSLATION.

"Let your laughter be turned to grief and your gladness to dejection. Humble yourselves in the presence of the Lord, and He will exalt you."

James 4:11.

"Speak not evil of one another, brethren. He that speaks evil of *his* brother and judges his brother, speaks evil of the law, and judges the law; but if you judge the law, you are not a doer of the law but a judge."

Speak not evil (mē katalaleīte). The usage is with *(mē)*. *Not.* Action in process must stop. *One another (állēlōn). Plural.* It is used as a reciprocal pronoun. Believers are to strive for good will and harmony in the church.

Brethren (ádelphoí). Fellow believers. There is an admonition for "Unity, one spirit, one mind, one accord" (Ps. 133:1-3; Phil. 1:27; 2:2).

Speaking against a brother in a derogatory manner, is a great disservice to him. In olden days, such a person was called a "Backbiter." "The north wind drives away rain; so does an angry countenance a backbiting tongue" (Prov. 25:23).

Judges *(krinōn).* An exhortation is given against evil speaking and uncharitable judgment. *Speaks evil (katalalōn). Of (the) law (nómou).* Although there is no definite article, clearly, it is the the Law, not law in general.

To speak against a brother was to speak against the Law. The Law had been maligned, misinterpreted and misapplied. The Law was made out to be something, it wasn't (Lev. 19:16, 18). *Judge (krinōn). Pass judgment.*

The critical, judging brother doesn't put the Law into practice. He isn't a performer but a judge. When the erring brother, misinterpreted the Law, acted upon that misinterpreted and denounced others, he became a judge but not a performer of the Law.

TRANSLATION.

> *"Stop speaking against one another, brethren. He who speaks against his brother or passes judgment upon his brother, speaks against the Law and passes judgment upon the Law, your are not a doer of the Law but a judge."*

James 4:12.

"There is one lawgiver, who *is* able to save and to destroy. Who are you that judges another?"

One ('eîs); ('heîs). There is only one Lawgiver whose laws are of permanent significance. His judgments are true. He is Lord of life and death. A*ble (dunámenos). Has power. To save (sōzō). Deliver. Preserve. Make safe.*

Salvation is the work of God Who delivers the sinner from the guilt of sin, penalty of sin, preserves from the power of sin, from the presence of sin (II Cor. 1:10).

The foundation of salvation is the efficacious death of Christ on the Cross, providing abundant grace to all who believe. Salvation is all of God from its inception on earth to its glorious consummation in Heaven (Jonah 2:9; John 19:30).

To destroy (apóllumı). The emphasis is upon God's power to reckon with sin (Matt. 10:28). The person who judges his brother disobeys the Law, thus putting himself above it and treating it with contempt.

TRANSLATION.

"Only One is the Lawgiver and Judge, He who has power to save and destroy. But as for you, who are you who passes judgment upon another?"

James 4:13.

"Go to now, you that say, Today or tomorrow we will go into such a city, and continue there a year, and buy and sell, and get gain."

Go to now (áye nūn). Come now. You who say ('oì); (hoì); (légontes). You are saying. Today (Sēmeron). This day. Or tomorrow (ē aúrıon). We will go (poreusōmeth). To depart from here. Into such a city (eís tēnde tēn pólın). This city.

And (kaí). Gives a lively tone. It reveals the lightness and thoughtlessness of a careless spirit. *Continue(poiēsōmen). Spend time. Buy and sell (émporeusōmen). Travel. Trade. Get gain (kerdēsōınō). Acquire. Make money.*

Such arrogant confidence about the future, is denounced. "Boast not yourself of tomorrow; for you know not what a day may bring forth" (Prov. 27:1). It is foolish, indeed, to leave God out of one's planning.

It also forms the theme, perhaps, of the most satirical of the Lord's parable. The young, rich fool made future plans, failing to realize the tenure of life, wasn't his to decide. His plan came to a miserable end (Luke 18:18—23).

TRANSLATION.

"Come now, you who are saying, Today or tomorrow we will go into this city and will spend a year there and will trade (do business) and make money."

72

James 4:14.

"Whereas you know not what *shall be* on the morrow. For what *is* your life? It is even a vapor that appears for a little time, and then vanishes away."

Whereas (hostia). Nature. Know not (ouk epistamai). On the morrow (aŏrion). Tomorrow. Since man is an ordinary mortal, he cannot possibly know about tomorrow with his limited knowledge.

Here, there is a striking contrast between man's ignorance, with the consequent incertitude of what tomorrow may bring forth. God is in control. "I *am* the LORD, I change not; therefore, *you* sons of Jacob are not consumed" (Mal. 3:6).

For what (poia gar). Of what kind. Character. Life (zoē). It is (estin). You are. It is a stronger word: "You yourselves: so that any thing of yours, even your life, must share in the same instability and brevity."

Vapor (atmis). Mist. That (hē). Which. A little time (oligon). Short time. Life at the longest on planet earth, soon comes to an end.

Vanishes away (aphanizomen). Disappear. In our day, some people live to be one hundred and past. Moses said of an eighty-year-old, "Our life is soon cut off, and we fly away" (Ps. 90:10).

TRANSLATION.

"Of what character is your life? For it is even a vapor which appears for a short time and then disappears."

James 4:15.

"*For you ought* to say, If the Lord will, we shall live, and do this or that."

For (ánti). Instead. You ought to say (toū légein. ṻmās); (humās). If (ean). (vs. 14 above) was parenthetical, so at this point, the thought is taken up from (*vs.* 13). Plans should take into account, the brevity of life.

If the Lord (eán) (ó); (ho); the Kúrios). Will (thlēsēi). God's purpose. The believer shouldn't run ahead of God. *We shall live (zēsōmen).* Our lives are in God's hands. Life and action are both dependent upon the Lord's will.

Do this or that (toūto ēkeīno). The details of our life are directed by the Lord. "But they that wait upon *trust* the LORD shall renew *their* strength; they shall mount up with wings as eagles; they shall run, and not be weary; and they shall walk, and not faint" (Isa. 40:31).

Walking is the routine things of life; running the emergencies of life. We always need the Lord in either situation. Eagles wings speak of supernatural help (Ps. 103:5). Life's routines wear down the strongest of men Jas. 4:16.

"But now you rejoice in your boastings; all such rejoicing is evil."

But now (nūn. dè). You boast (kauchāsthe). Constantly. In your vauntings (én taîs. álazoneíais). An unfavorable sense

A boaster (álazōn). Vagabond. Quack. Self-deceived *(álazoneía).* It is foolish arrogance to engage such uncertainties. Act of glorying is good if for Christ but bad if for self (I Thess. 2:19).

Evil (ponērá). Wicked. Pernicious. It is evil in its highly injurious and destructive character. *Boasting* of this kind must be evil as it forgets God and unduly exalts self.

TRANSLATION.

"But now you are constantly glorying in your (empty) boastings."

James 4:17.

"Therefore, to him that knows to do good, and does it not, to him it is sin."

Therefore (oūn). Conclusion. To (him). Knowing (eidóti). Positive knowledge. Assurance. To do (poieîn). To be doing. Good (kalòn). Morally excellent. That which is morally excellent in its nature.

And does it not (mē poioūnti). Perform. It is in the case of personal interest. It is an individual responsibility of the Christian to be performing that which pleases the Lord.

To him it is sin hamartia áútō). Sin to him. For emphasis. It is (estin). Sin (hamartia). Missing the mark, most common word for *sin (*Rom. 3:23).

It is missing God's glory in the failure to lift up those around us who need encouragement. Even, a word or deed might bring forth good fruit. Deeds speak louder than words. Know what is right, and doing what is right, honors the Lord.

Sin in the N.T., is: ignorance (Acts 3:17), disobedience (Rom. 3:25), falling short of duty (Rom. 11:12), deviation (II Cor. 5:19), unrighteousness (II Cor. 6:14), transgression (Heb. 2:14; I John 3:4). This chapters closes by saying unused knowledge of one's Christian duty, is sin, the sin of omission.

TRANSLATION.

"Accordingly, to him who positively knows how to be doing good and is not doing the same, sin it is to him."

CHAPTER FIVE

James 5:1.

"Go to now you rich men and weep and howl for your miseries that shall come upon you."

Go to now (age nun). (vs. 13 above). *Come now. You rich men (ho ploúsios). A group. O! rich men. Mostly likely unsaved.* They abound in material resources. Merely, being rich doesn't bring condemnation. Abraham was rich in faith and goods works.

Judgment comes rather for yielding readily to the temptations, to which the rich are especially susceptible. Riches can bring a false sense of security and insatiable love of power (Luke 6:24).

Lincoln said, "To test a man's stamina, send him trials and trouble. To test his character, give him power."

"The riches of earth are as uncertain as life itself." It is sheer folly to trust in them or to be ensnared by their wicked temptations (I Tim. 6:17).

Weep (klaiō). It was found in a papyrus, fragment sentence, "I assure you that ever since you left me, I have been mourning, weeping." *Howl (ololúzovtes). Howling with grief. For (epi). Over.*

Your miseries (talaipōriais humōn). Hardships. Many times the rich are deceived. *That (tais). Shall come upon (éperchoménais). Coming upon (you). Futuristic. Prophetic meaning.*

TRANSLATION.

"Come now, O! rich men, weep and audibly, wailing aloud because of your miseries which are coming upon you."

James 5:2.

"Your riches are corrupted and your garments are moth-eaten."

Your (humōn). Genitive case. *Possession. Riches (ploutos). Wealth.* Sooner or later the uncertainty of material possessions, brings disappointment and sorrow to all who rely on them. Riches have wings.

Are corrupted (sesōpen). Have rotted. Because of the decaying, deteriorating nature of wealth, one ought not allow such to rob him of the benefits of God's grace, which is lavished upon all who trust the Lord Jesus as personal Savior. Believers are "Rich in faith and heirs of the kingdom" (Jas. 2:5).

Garments (himatia). Cloak. Mantle. Tunic. Moth- eaten (sētobrōta). Your fine clothes are moth-eaten. In the ancient world, garments were used as payment, presents, heirlooms. Paul said in his farewell speech to the elders in Ephesus, "I have coveted no man's silver, gold or apparel" (Acts 20:33).

Riches are built in the sinking sands of time, and washed away with flood waters of economic, turn downs and myriads of other hazards.

TRANSLATION.

"Your riches have rotted, and your garments are moth-eaten."

James 5:3.

"Your gold and silver are cankered, and the rust of them shall be a witness against you, and shall eat your flesh as it were fire. You have heaped treasure together for the last days."

Your (ho). Possession. Gold (chrusos). Silver (arguros). Cankered (katiōtai). Become rusted over completely. Rust (ios). The word is used in (*vs.* James 3:8) with reference to the tongue.

Material wealth is powerless to meet the need or satisfy the deepest desire of the soul (Luke 12:15—22). *Witness (marturion). Testimony (marturion);* common idiom (Matt. 8:4).

Against you humin). This rust shall eventually speak mightily as a testimony which cannot be contradicted. *Your flesh (tas sarkas).* in the day of judgment (Rev. 17:16).

Fire (pur). History shows at one time, the ungodly rich let their bodies revel in wealth, bedecking themselves with fine garments, ornamented with gold.

Regarding those bodies, the words of Jesus are echoed: "The whole body cast into Hell" (Matt. 5:29-30.) *The fire of Gehenna"* (Matt. 5:22; 10:28). *You treasured up (ethēsaursate). Accumulate. Lay up.*

Last (eschatology). Last time. Eschatology is the doctrine of last things. Days (hēmerais). Last days are the days of the Messiah, marked from His first coming, preceding His second coming. Some have set days and times, deceiving many along the way. "The rich didn't know that the last days were already present (II Tim. 3:1)."

A London newspaper ran a contest, seeking a definition of money. The winner said, "Money is an article of exchange, a passport to any place except Heaven, buying anything except happiness."

These days of grace, are the opportunity to lay up "Treasures in heaven where moth and rust do not corrupt" (Matt. 6:20).

TRANSLATION.

"Your gold and your silver have become rusted over completely, and their rust shall be a testimony against you, and shall eat your flesh like fire. You laid up treasure for the last days."

James 5:4.

"Behold, the hire of the laborers who have reaped down your fields, which is of you kept back by fraud, cries; the cries of them who have reaped, are entered into the ears of the Lord of Sabāoth (Hosts)."

Behold (ídoū). The interjection gives a peculiar vivacity to the style, bidding the hearer or reader to attend to what is being said—*Behold! See! Lo! The hire (ho misthos). Pay. Wages. Laborers (ergatōn). Agricultural Workers* (Matt. 9:37).

Reaped (ámēnsantōn). Harvest. Fields (chōras). A tract of land. The Jews were farmers before they were traders. It was a natural step as they gained wealth, acquiring land in the dispersion.

Which (ho). Has been kept back (apesterēmenos). By fraud (aph' humōn). Cries out (kazei). Against injustice.

Swindling the poor is forbidden (Deut. 24:14-15). The workers cry out for vengeance. Perfect tense show permanency of the problem.

Are entered (eiselēlutha). Have entered. Lord of Sabāoth. (Kuríos). Lord of Hosts. It refers to God's Omnipotence (*Pantokratōr*); (Rev.4:8). The Sovereign God sees the woeful mistreatment.

The Lord of Sabāoth highlights the Truth, though the poor and oppressed have no champion on earth. However, they have a Helper and Avenger—the Lord God Omnipotent! "God hears the cries of the oppressed, even if their employers are deaf.

One authority pointed out the tenses: "Two aorists participles indicate the complete mowing and reaping; a perfect participle shows the fact the wages were held back permanently. Quick action was needed to rectify the injustice.

A present tense indicated the continuous crying of the wages held back; a perfect tense, expressing the shouts that "Have entered the Lord's ears, ever seeking the Lord's help (Luke 11:8—10).

TRANSLATION.

"Behold, the pay of the workman who mowed your fields which has been kept back by you, cries out; the cries of those who reaped, have entered into the ears of the Lord of Hosts."

James 5:5.

"You have lived in pleasure on the earth, and been wanton; you have nourished your hearts, as in a day of slaughter."

You have lived in pleasure (éthéruphēsate). Lived delicately. The words tell of a soft, luxurious life-style and self-indulgence. The *rich man* "Fared sumptuously every day" (Luke 16:19). Earth (gēs).

Wanton (éspatalēsate). It was a voluptuous life, in the sense of giving one's self to extravagant waste. The Prodigal Son scattered his substance in riotous, wasteful living (Luke 15:13). *Nourished (éthrepsate). Fatten (*Matt.6:26).

Hearts (kardías). The *heart* is the center, seat of thoughts, affections, purposes and endeavors of the inner man. The aorist declares the whole past is reviewed as on a judgment day. *In (en). Position. Slaughter (sphgēs). Description.* These, luxurious people will be revealed in self-indulgence on the day of judgment.

Our Lord said, "They ate, they drank...and the flood came and destroyed them all...after the same manner, it shall be in the day when the Son of man is revealed" (Luke 17:27, 30). The day of reckoning comes on apace.

TRANSLATION.

"You led a soft and luxurious life (of ease and self-indulgence) upon the earth, and gave yourselves to pleasure (characterized by extravagant waste); you fattened your hearts in a day of slaughter."

James 5:6.

"*You* have condemned *and* killed the just; *and* he does not resist you."

Condemned katedikásate). Give judgment against. Announce guilty. The rich controlled the courts of justice, which were used as instruments of oppression, initially, putting the righteous at a disadvantage. The rich are exposed for condemning the innocent righteous or just ones.

Killed the just (éphoneúsate). Murder. This was the practice of the rich, taking the poor, the righteous, to court to take away what little they might have, hence, in a sense, murdering them.

The just or righteous person has been declared righteous on the basis of the redemption in Christ Jesus, a Christian (Rom. 3:24; II Cor. 5:21). Just, upright, righteous are from (*dikaios*).

Resist (ántitássetai). Range in battle against. This is a vivid picture of the righteous of their patient acquiescence in ill-treatment. *You (su).* They were guilty of condemning and murdering the righteous person whose behavior "Under persecution is ever that of meekness and submission" (Matt. 5:39-42).

The down-trodden was aware of the futility of resistance. However, their hopes were focused on the time to come, knowing their oppressors, have an inescapable appointment with God on judgment day (Acts 17:31).

TRANSLATION.

"You condemned, you murdered the righteous (person); he does not resist you."

James 5:7.

"Be patient therefore, brethren, unto the coming of the Lord. Behold, the husbandman waits for the precious fruit of the earth, and has long patience for it, until he receive the early and latter rain.

Patient (makrothumḗsate). Long spirit. There was a call for patience in waiting for the Lord's return, with an added though of His imminent coming, bearing the offenses and injuries of others.

Patiently, they were holding out under trials, a self-restraint, which doesn't retaliate a wrong. The word was used of God and man (Rom. 2:4; II Cor. 6:6). *Brethren (ádelphoí). Fellow-believers.*

Unto (heōs). Limit. Until. Coming (parousías). The meaning is to be present along side of one. It will take place at the Rapture of the church into the glory world. It could take place at any moment. De Haan had a plaque on his office desk, "Perhaps, to day."

At the Rapture, the Lord Jesus will descend into the atmosphere of the earth and catch away the church (I Thess. 4:13—18). We must "Watch, work and wait" (I Thess. 1:10). *The Lord (tou Kurion).* The Rapture will be pre-tribulational (I Thess. 5:9; Rev. 3:10).

Behold (ídoū). Observe. Consider. Husbandman (geōrgos). Farmer. Waits (ékdéchomai). Look for. Expect. It is eager expectation as in (I Thess. 1:10). *Precious (tímion). Of great price. Fruit (karpòn). Produce of the land generally.*

Such fruit is precious; life depends on it. The shed blood of Christ is precious, our only hope of redemption (I Pet. 1:19; Heb. 9:22). The word means that for which there is no substitute.

Patience. The Farmer is waiting, looking for the crop to mature. The Farmer needs patience. We are more certain our Lord will come again than the Farmer who looks for the harvest. Nothing will hinder Jesus' return in God's time.

He receive (lábēi). It. The land. Not the Farmer. Early (prōimon). Oct.-Nov. The latter rain (ópsimon). It is the vernal rain, which comes in the months of March- April, just before the harvest.

The fertility of Israel is so depend on rainfall. God is faithful in sending an early rain to germinate the grain. Then, He sends the late rain for harvest. God is faithful. The Lord Jesus will come again. We will be caught up to be in His, personal presence forever.

TRANSLATION.

"Be patient in bearing the offenses and injuries of others, therefore, brethren, until the coming of the Lord. Observe (how) the Farmer waits with eager expectation for the precious produce of the earth, exercising patience over it, until it (the earth) may receive an early and a late rain."

James 5:8.

"Be you also patient, establish your hearts; for the coming of the Lord draws nigh."

The importance of looking for Christ's return, is obvious in that repetition again challenges believers to remain assured in looking for the Rapture.

Patience (makrothumēsate). For the believer to remain calm, cool and collected, will give him an emotional uplift, knowing God will honor and keep His promises.

Establish (stērixate). Strengthen. Make firm. Christians are exhorted to remain firm in their hearts in view of our Lord's coming (Acts 1:9—11).

For spiritual victory, the believer must begin to exercise his soul, in looking for the Lord's return, yielding to the Holy Spirit for enabling grace, to render acceptable service in doing the will of God.

Draws nigh (ēggizō). Near. Perfect tense. The Lord "Has drawn near and is now at hand." "He went away, but not to stay, for He's coming back again." The Lord is always with us (Ps. 125:1-2).

TRANSLATION.

"As for you, you also be patient in bearing the offenses and injuries of others; strengthen your hearts because the coming of the Lord has drawn near and is now at hand."

James 5:9.

"Grudge not one against another, brethren, lest you be condemned: behold, the judge stands before the door."

Grudge not (mē stenazō). Groan. Murmur. "Stop groaning." Believers are urged to practice mutual forbearance in view of the Lord's coming. To cease from groaning, will promote harmony in the name of the Lord for the congregation.

When one is full of complaint, he is ready to grumble against even his best friends in an unreasonable manner. *Lest (hia). In order that. Condemned* (Matt. 7:1-5).

(The) *Judge (Kritēs). The Lord Jesus.* The erring Christian will be judged to restore fellowship with the Lord (John 5:22; I John 1:3). *Stands (histēmi).* (Matt. 24:33).

"The near approach of the Judge, is a motive for suspending the activity of our own judgment, as well as for deterring us from incurring speedy judgment on ourselves." *Against the doors (tōw thurōn hestēken).* Jesus the Judge is seen as ready for judgment.

TRANSLATION.

"Stop groaning, brethren, against one another, in order that you may not be judged. Behold, the Judge has taken His stand before the doors."

James 5:10.

"Take, my brethren, the prophets who have spoken in the name of the Lord, for an example of suffering afflictions, and of patience."

Take (lambanō). Appropriate. The Prophets (tous prophētas). A Prophet spoke to man for God. From their example of ill-treatment, believers would be encouraged to be patient in trials.

Who have spoken (hoi alalēsan). Speak. (legō). The Prophets spoke what they received from the Lord by inspiration (II Tim. 3:16; II Pet. 1:21). *Name (anomati). Divine Majesty. Perfection.*

A Priest represented man to God. Jesus is Prophet, Priest and Potentate, His Redemptive Offices (Luke 1:76; Heb. 3:1; Rev. 19:16). A king rules over man under God.

Example (hupodigm). Figure. Copy. Suffering afflictions (kakopathias). Believers are here reminded that afflictions, should bring patience. Suffering has always been the lot of God's servants.

"There has no temptation taken you but such as is common to man: but God is faithful, who will not suffer you to be tempted above that you are able, but will with the temptation also make a way to escape, that you might be able to bear it" (I Cor. 10:13). *Escape (ekbasin). A landing place.*

TRANSLATION.

> *"Take the prophets who spoke in the Lord's Name, brethren, as an example of suffering and of patience in bearing the offenses and injuries of others."*

James 5:11.

"Behold, we count them happy which endure. You have heard of the patience of Job, and have seen the end of the Lord; that the Lord is pitiful and of tender mercy."

Happy (makarízomĕn). Spiritual happiness. Endure (hupoménē). The meaning is to persevere under misfortune and trials. The believer must trust the Lord for deliverance from besetting trials.

Have heard (ákouō). Actually, Job was far from patient with his so-called comforters: Eliphaz (Job 4:1); Bildad (8:1); Zophar (11:1). Job did complain, but he refused to deny his faith in God (Job 2:10; 19:25-26). Job became an illustration of loyal endurance.

Behind the scene, Satan said that Job wouldn't serve God if trials, troubles and loss of family, came to afflict him (Job 1:11). God had identified Job as a faithful servant. All the heartaches had come from Satan. Satan was proved wrong and a liar. Beyond the trials, God blessed Job greatly (Job 42:12—17).

The end (to telos). The end refers to the closing experience which came to Job by God's command. Beyond the trials, God blessed Job abundantly.

Very pitiful (polúsplagchnós). Very kind. Tender mercy (oiktipmōn). Job had long experienced the severity of God, in the test of his character in the furnace of setbacks. In the end, God showed Himself to be "Very pitiful and of tender mercy" (Ps. 103:8).

Another word for mercy is (eleos). *Loyal love.* "And I will betroth you unto me forever; yea, I will betroth you unto me in righteousness, and in judgment, and in loving kindness, and in mercies" (Hos. 2:19).

God is Omniscient; He cannot make a mistake. God is Omnipotent; He cannot be defeated. God is Omnipresent; He is always with us.

TRANSLATION.

"(Now), Behold, we account those who endure misfortunes and trials, blessed and spiritually happy. You heard of Job's endurance of trials, and saw the end of the Lord, that the Lord is full of pity and compassion."

James 5:12.

"But above all things, my brethren, swear not, neither by heaven, neither by earth, neither by any other oath: but let your Yes be Yes; and *your* No be No; lest you fall into condemnation."

But above all things (de pantōn). Before (prò). Before the readers do anything else, they must stop using oaths, taking the Name of God in vain. *Swear not (mē ómnuō). Affirm with an oath. Stop swearing.*

A Christian speaking what he means, ought to be enough in getting words across to another. Nothing more is needed to establish communication. So many believers think something must be added.

Solemn statements made under oath in a court of law, involving, perhaps, one's life, are not the thought here. Levity is forbidden, when one might foolishly take God's Name in vain, as impatience and self-consciousness, were ignored.

Heaven (tòn oúranón). The Heaven. "The Jews were want to split hairs in their use of profanity. By avoiding the Name of God, imagined they were not guilty of this sin."

"Today, professing Christians use pious oaths that violate the prohibition of Jesus (Matt.5:34—36). Oaths in our conversation, are not a mild and excusable habit, even when omitting God's Name."

Yea (ētō). Yes. Nay (oú). No. Summary negation. It strengthens the thought. A simple statement ought to be enough, without embellishing it with one oath after the other. *Condemnation (hupókpιósιn). Act of judgment but not the sentence.* Christians are exhorted to stop putting themselves under oath in ordinary conversation.

TRANSLATION.

"But before all, my brethren, stop swearing, neither by Heaven, nor by the earth, nor by any other oath, but constantly be letting your Yes be Yes and your No be No in order that you may not fall under judgment."

James 5:13.

"Is any among you afflicted? Let him pray. Is any merry? Let him sing psalms."

Among you (én humīn). Association. Fellowship. Afflicted (kakopatheī, vs.10 above). *To suffer evils. Hardships. Continuous action.*

The reference is to O.T. Prophets and their trials, as they spoke in the Name of God, which constantly confronted them. Today, Christians face many evils in their pilgrim journey and walk of faith.

Let him pray (proséuchesthō). Let him offer prayers to God continually. "Pray without ceasing" (I Thess. 5:17). Prayer may not remove the affliction, but it certainly can transform it. The Christian is admonished to pray and rejoice in the midst of affliction.

Is anyone cheerful (tis eúthumeī); (Acts 27:22, 25). Let him s*ing psalms (psallō). Praise generally* (Eph. 5:19). Singing lifts the emotions and heart to a high mountain of praise. "Suffering should be the cause for prayer and happiness the reason."

Psallō must be given a wider reference for singing praises to God. It can be singing alone, vocally with or without accompaniment or other renditions.

TRANSLATION.

"Is any (believer) suffering hardship? Let him be praying continually. Is any (believer) cheerful? Let him be singing praises."

James 5:14.

"*Is* any sick among you? Let him call for the elders of the church; and let them pray over him, anointing him with oil in the name of the Lord."

Sick (àstheneō). Feeble. It refers to some, specific, bodily ailment or distress. Let him call for the Elders *(proskaleō).*

The *Elders (toùs presβutérous).* They were the Leaders (I Tim. 5:17; I Pet. 5:1, 5. *Of the church (tēs ékklēsías).* The Pastor would also pray for the sick. *Over him (ep' auton).*

A local, church, N.T. Church, in a specific place, is made up of regenerated, baptized believers, saved by the grace of God, meeting regularly together to worship, preach the gospel and observe the ordinances (I Cor. 1:2).

Anointing him (álephō). With oil (élaíōi). Many strange interpretations have come from this verse of Scripture. Olive oil was one of the best remedial known to the ancients.

In this setting, we have God and medicine, God and the Doctor. That is where we are today. Many physicians believe in God and want the help of prayer.

In the name of the Lord (én tōi ánómatı toū Kuríos). God may heal through answer to prayer, as here, or by medicine. The oil is the symbol of the presence of the LORD (Ps. 23:5). Ryrie said, "Prayers of faith are answered not simply because they are prayed in faith, but if they are prayed in the will of God" (I John 5:14).

TRANSLATION.

"Is any (believer) sick among you? Let him call immediately for the Elders of the (local) church; and let them pray over him, having anointed him with oil, in the Name of the Lord."

James 5:15.

"And the prayer of faith shall save the sick, and the Lord shall raise him up; and if he has committed sins, they shall be forgiven him."

The Prayer (hē eùchē). Prayer is a privilege and a responsibility. Moses spoke with the Lord, and the Lord spoke with Moses at the mercy seat. It was a meeting of hallowed fellowship (Num. 7:89). Prayer is asking and receiving in the will of God.

The faith (tēs písteōs). Prayer is offered in faith. *Save (sōsei).* It is the healing of the body and/or emotional, not salvation of the soul. The ill will be made well, whole, in answer to prayer. The verse doesn't allow for extreme unction or so-called, faith healers.

The Lord (ho Kúrios). Shall raise him up (égereî aútòn). The sick will raise up. He will recover in the blessing of the Lord. The application of oil soothes the body; the prayer comforts and strengthens the mind and soul by placing the patient into the hands of the Lord.

There is the exercise of faith and confidence in the gracious will of God that He will restore the sick to renewed health and strength. With or without means, all healing is of God.

(One who has) *committed sins (pepoiēkòs hamarías).*

Sin is missing the mark—of God's glory *(*Rom. 3:23). *It shall be forgiven him (áphethēsetai aútōi).* The blessing rests upon the believer's confession (I John 1:9).

TRANSLATION.

"And the prayer which faith offers shall make the sick believer well, and the Lord will raise him up. And if he is in a condition of having committed sin, it shall be forgiven him."

James 5:16.

"Confess *your* faults one to another, and pray one for another, that you may be healed. The effectual prayer of a righteous man avails much."

Confess your faults (èxomologeîsthe tà paraptōmata).(your); (*Offenses). To one another (állélois).* Confession of sin to God is already assumed. The context shows a believer, making things right with one another and restoring fellowship (Matt. 5:23, 24). Were believers requesting prayer for besetting sins?

And p*ray for one another (kaì eúchesthe hupér állélois). That you may be healed (hópōs ìathēte).* This healing would be physical, as well as release from ill-feeling or grudge toward another believer. This would be a blessing to Christians and the church as well.

The effectual fervent prayer of a righteous man avails much (*énergouménē déēsis dikaíou polù ìschúei). (*The, *operative supplication of a righteous (*man) *prevails much).*

When the heart is right and the condition is met, God delights to answer prayer. "The *Righteous man* is a believer. Ryrie stated, "The righteous man knows how to pray in the will of God."

Great blessings awaits the church, where believers will get right with one another and pray for each another. There will be touch of Heaven upon the congregation. Thankfully, I saw such an outpouring.

TRANSLATION.

"Be confessing your sins to one another, and be praying for one another that you may be healed."

James 5:17.

"Elias was a man subject to like passions as we are, and he prayed earnestly that it might not rain: and it rained not upon the earth by the space of three years and six months."

Elias (Elijah). His name means "My God is Jehovah." He has been well entitled the greatest prophet that ever came out of Israel. He was Elijah the Tishbite of Gilead (I Kig. 17:1).

Man (ánthrōpos). Human like ourselves. Subject to like passions to us (homoιopathès hēmīn). Like feelings to us. And with prayer he prayed (kaì proseuchēi proséúxato). (For it) Not to rain (toū mè βréxai). And it did not rain upon the earth (kaì oúk ἔβrexen épì tēs gēs).

Elijah is like *our nature and constitution* (Acts 14:15). The magnitude of his achievements, are contrasted with his "ups-and-downs" of his very human character.

He was bold as a lion on Mount Carmel in denouncing Ahab and false prophets; yet, he sank low in despondency and distrust on Mount Horeb. He was a spiritual giant for God in getting his prayers answered in demonstration of God power.

Prayed (proséuchē). With prayer. He prayed (proséuxato). In classical Greek, it is an idiom for intensity that he prayed, prayingly. *Not to rain (tou mē βrexai). And it did not rain (kaì oúk ἔbrexen). Three years and six months (eniautous treis kai mēnas hex).*

TRANSLATION.

"Elijah was a man of like nature to us, and he prayed fervently that it might not rain upon the earth for three years and six months."

James 5:18.

"An he prayed again, and the heaven gave rain, and the earth brought forth her fruit."

He prayed (proseúxato). Offer prayers. The Heaven (ho oùranòs). God gave rain (*God édōken hutòn*). It is an historical truth God answered Elijah's prayer in giving rain. *Brought forth (éßlastēsen). Her fruit (aútēs karpòn). Its fruit.* God's power in prayer was a rebuke to a wayward nation.

TRANSLATION.

"And again he prayed and the Heaven (God) gave rain, and the earth brought forth its fruit."

James 5:19.

"Brethren, if any of you do err from the truth, and one convert him."

Brethren (ádelphoì). If (eán). Hypothetical situation. Any (tıs). Anyone. Believer. Of you (èn humīn). Among you. Do err (planēthēi). Go astray. Wander. From (ápò). Away from. The Truth (tēs álētheís). The Word of God. The gospel (vss. 1:18; 3:14).

Convert him (epıstrépsēi). Cause him to return to the Lord. *Bring* back (Luke 22:32). *Him (auton). A*nyone (tis). A believer who is out of fellowship with the Lord. The Christian has wandered far from God. There is prayer for and hope that he will return to the Lord for blessing and fellowship (I Cor. 1:9).

There must be constant watchfulness, lest the things of God become common place or routine. We need to encourage and pray for one another to stay on the pilgrim pathway (Prov. 3:5—7).

TRANSLATION.

*"My brethren, if any (believer) among you wanders away from
the Truth and any (believer) brings him back."*

James 5:20.

"Let him know, that he who converts the sinner from the error of his way shall save a soul from death, and shall hide a multitude of sins."

Let him know (gınōskétō). Know constantly. Converts.

And brings back a sinner from (the) error of his way (hóti ho épıstpépas hamartōlòn ék plánēs hodoū aútoū).

Shall save (sōsei). A soul from death (psuchēn (ék thanátou). And shall hide kalúpseı). Multitude (plēthos). Of sins (hamartıōn). The erring brother came back to the Lord for the delight and great encourage of all, especially to everyone who prayed and sought him.

The death is physical (I Cor. 11:30). The Christian cannot die any other kind of death because of his permanent relationship with God through grace.

An erring brother who persists in his waywardness, subjects himself to the judgment of the Lord. In the believer's return to the Lord, it is quiet obvious how a multitude of sins would never occur.

TRANSLATION.

*"Let him be constantly knowing that he who has brought back
a sinner back from the error of his way, shall save his soul from
death and shall cover up a great number of sins."*

El Finis

THE ENLARGED TRANSLATION

The Enlarged Translation has been arranged in a paragraph format so that the reader may get the flow of thought of the inspired Epistle from beginning to end. Let us remembering that the Word of God is our only source of spiritual strength and power.

"All scripture is given by inspiration of God, and is profitable for doctrine, for reproof, for correction, for instruction in righteousness. That the man of God might be thoroughly furnished (*equipped*) unto all good works" (II Timothy 3:16-17).

CHAPTER ONE

1-1

James of God and of the Lord Jesus Christ a bond- servant to the twelve tribes who are in the dispersion.

2-8

For yourselves, my brethren, consider it now, once and for all, all joy whenever you may fall into the midst of various trials. Continually, knowing by experience that the proving of your faith is for yourselves, my brethren, consider it now, once accomplishing endurance. But let endurance, be having its perfect (finished) *work, in order that you may continually be mature and wholly complete, lacking in nothing. But if, as is the case, any of your be destitute of wisdom, let him be asking in the sphere of faith, nothing doubting. For he who is constantly doubting, is like a wave of the sea continually driven and tossed (*about*). For let not that man be supposing that he shall receive anything from the Lord. A double soul man, (torn by conflicting desires), is unstable in all his ways* (in his whole manner of life).

9-12

*But let the brother, the lowly one, be glorying in his exaltation. But the rich in his low estate (*humiliation*), because as the flower of grass he shall pass away (*completely*). For the sun rises with the burning heat and dries up the grass and its flower falls off, and the beauty of its appearance perishes; so also the wealthy* (man) *in his goings,* (pursuits) *shall wither* (away). *Spiritually prosperous is the man who is constantly enduring temptation, because when he has been approved, he shall receive the crown of life, which He* (the Lord) promised to those who are loving Him.

13-15
(When) *being tempted, let no one be saying, From God, as a source, I am being tempted, for God is incapable of being tempted by things evil in nature; indeed, He Himself is tempting no one. But each one is being tempted by his own* (lustful) *desire, when he is being drawn away and is being enticed. Then the* (lustful) *desire having conceived, is bringing forth sin, and the sin, having been fully completed, is giving birth to death.*

16-18
Stop being deceived, my brethren, divinely loved ones. Every good gift and every perfect gift is from above, coming down form the Father of lights (heavenly bodies), *with Whom there can be no variation* (change) *nor shadow that is cast by turning. Because He* (God) *deliberately willed it. He gave a* (spiritual) *birth by means of the Word of Truth, resulting in our being a kind of first-fruits of His creatures*

19-25
You know absolutely, my beloved brethren. Now, let every man practice being quick to hear, slow to speak and slow to wrath. For a man's wrath does not result in that which is righteous in the sight of God. Wherefore, having put off and away from yourselves every moral defilement and abundance of malice, in meekness welcome and appropriate the implanted Word which has power to save your souls. Now, keep on becoming doers of the Word and not hearers only, constantly, cheating yourselves by false reasoning. Because if, assuming that, anyone is a hearer of the Word and not a doer; this one is like a man attentively considering the face of his birth in a mirror. For, he takes a look at himself and off he has gone, and immediately, completely forgot what sort of (a man) *he was. But he who has looked into the perfect Law, the Law of Liberty, and has always continued* (in it), *not having become a hearer of forgetfulness but a doer of work, this man shall be blessed* (spiritually).

26-27

If, assuming that, anyone supposes himself to be religious, not bridling his tongue but deceiving his own heart, this person's religion is useless. Religion (which is) pure, and unsoiled before God, even the Father, is this: to visit and look after orphans and widows in their distress, (and) to practice keeping one's self, without spot, from the world.

CHAPTER TWO

1-4

My, brethren, stop holding the faith in our Lord Jesus Christ, (the Lord) *of the glory, in connection with showing partiality to persons. For if there comes into your synagogue* (meeting place), *a man with gold rings on his hand in shining clothing, and here comes in also a poor, beggarly man in dirty clothing, and you look with admiration upon the one wearing the shining clothing and say, You, be sitting down here in this seat of honor, and say to the poor, beggarly man, as for you, take a stand in that place or be sitting down beside my footstool; are you not divided in your own mind and have become judges with wicked thoughts?*

5-7

Listen, my beloved brethren! Did not God choose out for Himself the poor with reference to the world, rich in faith and heirs of the kingdom which He promised those loving Him? As for you, you yourselves dishonored the, poor, beggarly man. Do not the wealthy work harm against you, and they themselves drag you off into the courts of law? Do not they themselves speak reproachfully of the noble name (Christian) *which was put upon* (by the Lord)?

8-13

If you really fulfill the royal law according to the Scripture, you shall love your neighbor as yourself, you are doing excellently. But if, assuming that, *you are showing partiality (*to the wealthy*), you are committing sin, being convicted by the Law as transgressors. For, whoever shall observe the whole law, but shall stumble in one single (*point*), he has become (*and is*) guilty of all. For, He who said, Do not commit adultery, also said, Do not commit murder. Now if, assuming that, you are not committing adultery but are committing murder, you have become a transgressor of the Law. In such a manner, be speaking and in such a manner be habitually doing, as those who are about to be judged by means of the Law of Liberty. For the judgment will be without mercy to him who did not exercise mercy; mercy triumphs over judgment.*

14-17

*What is the profit, my brethren, if any one is saying, That he has faith and has not works? That faith (*without works*) is not able to save him, is it? But if a brother or sister have been without sufficient clothing for some time and are lacking in daily food, and one of you say to them, Be going away in peace, be warming yourselves and be feeding yourselves, but you do not give them the things needful to the body, what is the profit? Thus, also the faith, if it does not keep on constantly having works, is dead in itself.*

18-19

But someone will say, As for you, you have faith, and as for myself, I have works. Show me, at once, your faith apart from works, and I will show you my faith by my works. As for you, you believe God is one. You are doing well. The demons also believe and tremble.

20-23

*But do you wish to come to know, O empty man, that the faith apart from works, is (*barren, idle*)? Was not Abraham our Father vindicated by works, when he offered Isaac his son on the altar of sacrifice? You see that the faith was working with his works, and by works his faith was complete. And the Scripture was realized in every particular which says, And Abraham believed God, and is was reckoned to him for righteousness, and a friend of God, he was called.*

24-26

You see that by works a man is declared righteous and not by faith alone. And, in like manner, also was not Rabab, the harlot, vindicated by works in that she secretly received as guests the messengers and thrust them forth by means of a different way? For just as the body apart from the spirit, is dead, so also the faith apart from its works, is dead.

CHAPTER THREE

1-6

*Stop becoming many teachers, my brethren, knowing positively that we shall receive the greater sentence of judgment. For, with reference to many things, we all stumble. If anyone does not stumble in word, this one is a mature, Christian man, able to restrain also his whole body. Now, if such being the case, we put bridles in the mouths of horses in order that they may be obeying us; also, we turn about (*guide*) their whole body. Behold, also the ships, though they are so great and are driven by violent winds, are turned about by a very small rudder, wherever the impulse of the steersman deliberately wills. Thus, also the tongue is a small member and boasts great things. Behold, how great a forest a little fire sets aflame. And the tongue is a fire, that world marked by iniquity. The tongue is so established in our members that it defiles the whole body and sets on fire the wheel (*whole round) of existence and is continually being set on fire by Gehenna.*

7-12

*For, every nature of beasts, quadrupeds and birds and reptiles and marine life, is tamed and has been tamed by the nature of man. But the tongue no one of man has power to tame. (It is) a restless evil, full of death-bringing poison. By means of it we bless the Lord, even the Father, and by means of it we curse (*imprecate evil on) men who have been made in the image of God. Out of the same mouth comes forth blessing and cursing. My brethren, these things ought not thus to keep* *on constantly taking place. The spring out of the same opening does not gush forth the sweet and the bitter, does it? A fig tree, my brethren, does not have power to produce olives, does it? Or a vine, figs? Neither, does salt* (water) *have power to produce sweet water*

13-18

Who is wise and understanding among you? Let him exhibit out of a good (and excellent) *manner of life his works in meekness of* (true) *wisdom. But if, such being the case, you are having bitter jealousy and rivalry* (faction and party spirit) *in your heart, stop constantly boasting and lying against the Truth. This wisdom is not one coming down from above, but is earthly, sensual* (non-spiritual), *demon-like. For, where jealousy and rivalry exist, there is restlessness and every kind of base* (wicked, bad) *deed. But the wisdom from above is first* (essentially) *pure, then peaceable, reasonable, compliant, full of mercy and good fruits, impartial, free from hypocrisy* (insincerity). *And the fruit of righteousness is sown in peace for those making peace.*

CHAPTER FOUR

1-4

From what source are quarrels and fights among you? Do they not come out of your sinful pleasures which are constantly campaigning in your members? You have a yearning desire for, and you do not possess; you kill. And you boil with envy and anger, and you are not able to obtain. You quarrel and fight. You have not because you ask not, praying for something to be given you and do not receive because you pray with evil intent for something to be given in order that you may spend it in your sinful pleasures. O! Adulteresses, do you not know with positive assurance that your friendship with the world, is enmity with God? Whoever, therefore, would purpose deliberately to be a friend of the world, establishes (himself) *as an enemy of God*

5-10

Or, do you think that the Scripture speaks to no purpose, the (Holy) *Spirit Who has been caused to take up His permanent home in us, has an earnest desire* (for complete sway over us) *to* (the degree of) *jealous envy? Moreover, He* (the Holy Spirit) *gives greater grace. On which account, He* (the Holy Spirit) *says, God sets Himself in array against the proud and haughty but gives grace to the humble and lowly. Accordingly, be obedient with complete subjection to God. Stand against the Devil, and he will flee away from you. Draw near to God, and He will draw near to you. Cleanse* (your) *hands, O! Sinners and purify* (your) *hearts, O!*

Doubled-soul. Be miserably afflicted, mourn and cry aloud. Let your laughter be turned to grief and your gladness to dejection. Humble yourselves in the presence of the Lord, and He will exalt you.

11-12

Stop speaking against one another, brethren. He who speaks against his brother, speaks against the Law and judgment upon the Law. Now, if you pass judgment upon the Law, you are not a doer of the Law but a judge. Only one is the Lawgiver and Judge, He who has power to save and to destroy. But, as for you, who are you who passes judgment upon his brother?

13-17

Come now, you who are saying, Today or tomorrow, we will go into this city and will spend a year there and will trade (do business) *and make money. You are of such a nature that you do not know what shall be tomorrow. Of what character is your life? For you are a vapor which appears for a short time and then disappears. Instead of your saying, If the Lord wills, we shall both live and do this or that. But now, you are constantly glorying in your* (empty) *boasting. All such glorying is wicked. Accordingly, to him who positively knows how to be doing good and is not doing the same, to him, it is sin.*

CHAPTER FIVE

1-6

Come now, O rich man, weep audibly, wailing aloud because of your miseries which are coming upon you. Your riches have rotted and your garments have become moth-eaten. Your gold and your silver have become rusted over completely, and their rust shall be a testimony against you, and shall eat your flesh as fire. You laid up treasures in the last days. Behold, the pay of the workman who mowed your fields which have been held back, cries out; and the cries of those who have reaped, have entered into the ears of the Lord of Hosts. You led a soft and luxurious life (of ease and self-indulgence) *upon the earth, and gave yourselves* (characterized by extravagant waste); *you fattened your hearts in a day of slaughter. You condemned, you murdered the righteous* (person); *he does not resist you.*

7-9

Be patience in bearing the offenses and injuries of others, therefore, brethren, unto the coming of the Lord. Observe (how) *the Farmer waits with eager expectation for the precious fruit of the earth, exercising patience over it, until it* (the earth) *may receive an early and a late rain. As for you, you also be patient in bearing the offenses and injuries of others; strengthen your hearts because the coming of the Lord has drawn near and is now at hand. Stop groaning, brethren, against one another, in order that you may not be judged. Behold, the Judge* (Jesus) *has taken a stand before the doors.*

10-11

Take the prophets who spoke in the Name of the Lord, brethren, as an example of suffering and of patience in bearing the offenses and injuries of others. (Now), behold, we account those who endure misfortunes and trial, spiritually blessed. You heard of the endurance of Job in trials, and saw the end of the Lord, that He is full of pity and compassion.

12

Above all things, my brethren, stop swearing, neither by the Heaven, nor by the earth, nor by any other oath, but be letting your Yes be Yes and your No be No in order that you may not fall under judgment.

13-15

Is any (believer) *among you suffering hardship? Let him be constantly praying. Is any* (believer) *cheerful? Let him be singing praises. Is any* (believer) *sick among you? Let him call immediately for the Elders of the (*local*) church; and let them be praying over him, having anointed him with olive oil, in the Name of the Lord. And the prayer which faith offers shall make the sick believer well, and the Lord shall raise him up. And if he is in a condition of having committing sin, it shall be forgiven him.*

16-18

Be confessing, therefore, your sins to one another, and be praying for one another that you may be healed. The prayer of a righteous man (believer) *avails much (*has much force*) in its working. Elijah was a man of like nature to us, and he prayed fervently that it might not rain, and it did not rain for three years and six months. And he prayed again, and the Heaven (*God*) gain rain, and the earth produced its fruit.*

19-20

My, brethren, if any (believer) *among you wanders away form the Truth and any (*believer*) brings him back; let him be constantly knowing that he who has brought back a sinner (believer) out of his wandering ways, shall save a soul (*believer*) from death (physical) and shall cover a great number of sins.*

APPENDIX I

DWIGHT LYMAN MOODY

(1837-1999)

Moody said, "Before he learned the secret of the Holy Spirit, he was like a man with a barrel of water on his back."

Afterwards, he was like a man swimming in deep waters.

Water out of the Temple river was up to the ankles; then, to the knees, loins and water to swim in, a river that couldn't be passed over (Ezekiel 47:3—5).

God used Moody mightily in great, soul winning conferences in America, England and beyond.

"God bless the school that D.L. Moody founded."

In Chicago!

APPENDIX II

FRANK DOUBLEDAY

(1862-1934)

Publisher Frank Doubleday had a one-of-a-kind book that was bound in red Russian leather. He called it the book of the law and the profit. Unlike the portions of the Bible that we call the Law and the Prophets, Doubleday's book was an account of his business dealings and his financial profits.

According to author, George Doran, the red book contained Doubleday's morning prayers and evening vespers. In other words, it seemed that he worshiped money.

Jesus knew how easily all of us are tempted to become devotees of money and all the things it can buy. He warned, "No man can serve two masters...You cannot serve God and mammon (money)" (Matthew 6:24).

We are idolaters if we put our trust in money as the ultimate source of our security and happiness. Our Lord also warned against being absorbed in the things that gratify our fleshly desires and self-centered ambitions. He asked, "What profit is it to man if he gained the whole world, and lose his own soul?" (16:26).

Money can't bring us true and lasting profit. That can be found only by trusting the living God (I Timothy 6:17). As we put our hope in Him and live in obedience to His Word, we will have eternal life profit (*vs.* 10). —Grounds

If I gain the world but not the Savior,
Would my gain be worth the lifelong strife?
Are all earthly pleasures worth comparing
For a moment with a Christ-filled life?
                    —Olander

Appendix III

John D. Rockeffer

(1839-1937)

Reading in Genesis 6:14, "Make you an ark of gopher wood; rooms shall you make in the ark, and shall pitch it within and without with pitch, Rockefeller reasoned, "Where there is pitch, there is oil." He founded Standard oil Company.

Rockefeller with chauffeured limousine, gave children rides on Sunday afternoons in Manhattan. He stopped at a curb and asked a girl if she would like to go for a ride? She asked, "Where are you going?" "Heaven"! She said, "Know you aren't; you don't have enough gasoline.

Rockefeller had a heart attack at forty-four. His Doctor put him on water and crackers. He began to give his money away and lived to be eighty-eight. Rockefeller said, "As I study wealthy men I can see but one in which they can secure a real equivalent for money spent, and that is to cultivate a taste for giving where the money may produce an effect which will be a lasting gratification."

APPENDIX IV

THE LITTLE MEMBER

"Even the tongue is a little member, and boasts great things. Behold, how great a little fire kindles" (Jas. 3:5).

The larger context: James 3:1—18).
INTRO.
The potential of the tongue may reach the highest mountain of delight or sink to the lowest valley of discouragement.

OUTLINE
Helpful Tongue.
    A. Promotes church unity.
        "Only let your conversation (conduct) be as it becomes the gospel of Christ, that whether I come and see you, or else be absent, I may hear of your affairs, that you stand fast in one spirit, with one mind striving together for the faith of the gospel" (Phil. 1:27).
    B. Present a testimony.
        "Jesus saith...Go home to your friends, and tell them how great things the Lord has done for you, and has had great compassion on you. And he departed, and began to publish (proclaim) in Decapolis how great things Jesus had done for him: and all men did marvel" (Mark 5:19-20).

C. Worship the Lord.

"My tongue shall sing aloud of your righteousness" (Ps. 51:14).

D. The tongue a tree of life.

"A wholesome tongue is a tree of life" (Prov. 15:4).

II. Hurtful Tongue.

A. Wisdom or anger (Prov. 15:1).

B. Guile and evil.

"Keep your tongue from evil, and your lips from guile *(deceit)* (Ps. 34:13).

C. Two membes in a church talked on the telephone for 4 1/2 hours and wanted the people to know about it. "In the multitude of words there wants not sin: but he that refrains (restrains) his lips *is* wise" (Prov. 10:19).

D. Death and life in the tongue. "Death and life are in the power of the tongue: and they that love it shall eat the fruit thereof" (Prov. 18:21).

E. The tongue is a sword.

"Who whets (sharpens) their tongue like a sword, *and* bend *their bows to shoot* their arrows, *even* bitter words?" (Ps. 64:3).

F. The tongue is a razor.

"The tongue devises mischief (destruction); like a sharp razor" (Ps. 52:2).

G. The lying tongue.

"A proud look, a lying tongue, and hands that shed innocent blood" (Prov. 6:17).

H. The perverse tongue.

"He that has a *(perverse)* heart finds no good; and he that has a perverse tongue falls into mischief" (Prov. 17:20).

I. The tongue spreads gossip.

"...The mouth of fools pours out foolishness" (Prov. 15:2).

III. THE HARNESSED TONGUE.

A. Often one hears, "Oh! My tongue gets me into so much trouble. How may I control it? Many times I feel that I must bite my tongue."

B. Many times we speak without thinking. Refrain from controlling the conversation or manipulating people.

C. Forgive (Eph. 4:32).

D. Restore a broken relationship.

E. Think positively.

F. Respect the other person.

G. Respect will eliminate many pitfalls.

H. Remember the explosive dynamic of the tongue to cause widespread harm.

I. Begin each day with prayer and Bible study, for the Lord will help you in controlling the uncontrollable tongue.

"Rumor is the art of saying nothing, while leaving nothing unsaid."

APPENDIX V

A LOCAL CHURCH

A local church in a specific place is composed of regenerated, baptized, band together for regular worship and the ministry of the gospel.

There are two servants who lead a church in doing the will of God: Pastors and Deacons. There is observant of two ordinances: Baptism and the Lord's Supper or Communion.

In obedience to the Great Commission, there is an outreach to local and world missions.

(Matt. 28:18—20; I Cor. 11:23—34; II Cor. 13:14;Eph. 1:1; 3:1—5; Heb. 10:35).

APPENDIX

Appendix VII

The Eight Greek Cases

I. Nominative: Case of the finite verb. **II.** Genitive: Case of possession. III.. Ablative: Case of separation. IV. . Instrumental: Case of means. **V.** Locative: Case of position. **VI.** Dative: Case of personal interest. **VII.** Accusative: Case of direct object. Vocative: Case of direct address.

APPENDIX VII

THE MONEY BAG

I can remember the experience so well even after many years. It took place in late Summer of 1958.

I was on a preaching mission in the small, rustic town of USA, Missouri, located about forty-five or so miles South/East of Jefferson City, Capital of the "Show-me state."

During the week of meetings, I stayed in the home of Robert and Robin Greenwood, in their guest room. I had some meals with them. I had other meals in homes of church people. (Names changed).

Mrs. Greenwood was a very kind and pleasant person who seemed to enjoy life and excellent hostess. My stay with them was most enjoyable, as well as, memorable in a number of ways.

Mr. Robert Greenwood , owner of the General Store, which had about everything needed in a rural community. He worked hard and long hours to make his store a success.

He was realizing a profit, managing his business. Robert let me know with an air of confidence money would solve a lot of problem and give some security in life.

On the Saturday of that week, the three of us gathered around the supper table (city folk: dinner). As table talk began, Robert let me know he had $2,500 in his possession from receipts of the day, giving him renewed security.

After supper, I went to church and afterwards to the Pastor's home for refreshments in accordance with after-church ritual. Usually, I returned to Greenwoods around 11:00 P.M.

Leaving the Pastor's home that evening, only a block away, I walked to the Greenwoods, across the porch and opened the front door. Entering the hallway, I was about ready to go up to the room.

Suddenly, Robert hollered out, "Don't take another step, or I'll shoot you dead." Frightened, almost beyond words, with my heart in my throat, I managed to get out a feeble reply, "Don't shoot, I'm the Preacher, going up to my room."

"Go ahead, I thought you were a robber after my money," said Greenwood in a rather embarrassed, subdued voice. I heard his wife say to him, "Sometime, your money is going to drive you out of your mind."

Regaining my composure and strength, I dashed up the stairs to my room and locked the door. With a sigh of relief, I was thankful to be alive, so that people wouldn't read in a paper: "Guest Preacher killed in a church-related situation."

After a little while, I dropped off to sleep until about 2:00 A.M. I was awakened by the loud talk of Greenwood with a neighbor, Otis Plum.

Greenwood said to his neighbor, "No! You take the money bag and pistol to your house so that I can get some sleep before daybreak."

BIBLIOGRAPHY

Alford. Henry, The Greek New Testament (Cambridge: Deighton, Bell, and Co., 1880). Vol. I.

Cambridge *Greek* *New* *Testament,* *The Epistle of James* (Cambridge: The University Press, 1905).

Creamer, Hermann, *The Biblico-Theological Lexicon* of *New Testament Greek* (Edinburgh Press, 1954).

Davis, William Hersey, Beginner's Greek Grammar of the Greek New Testament (Nashville: Broadman Press, 1923).

Lenski, R. G. H., *The Interpretation of the Epistle of Hebrews* and *The Epistle of James* (Columbus, Ohio: Wartburg Press, 1946).

Lineberry, John, *Salvation is of the Lord* (Grand Raids: Zondervan Pub. Co., 1959).

—-*Vital Word Studies in I Thessalonians* (Grand Rapids: Zondervan Pub. Co., 1960).

—-*Vital Word Studies in II Thessalonians* (Grand Rapids: Zondervan Pub. Co., 1961).

Milligan, George; Moulton, James (*The Vocabulary of the Greek Testament* (Grand Rapids: Eerdmans Pub. Co., 1957).

Peloubet's Bible Dictionary (Philadelphia: The John C. Winston Co., 1925).

Robertson, A.T., *Word Pictures in the New Testament.* (Nashville: Broadman Press, 1933). Vols., I & VI.

Tasker, R. V. G. *General Epistle of James* (London: Tyndale Press & Eerdmans (Grand Rapids: 1956).

Thayer, Joseph, *A Greek-English Lexicon of the New Testament* (New York: American Book Co., 1889).

The Expositor's Greek Testament, (Grand Rapids: Eerdmans Pub., Co.,). Vol. IV.

Vincent, Marvin R., *Word Studies in the New Testament* (Grand Rapids: The Eerdmans Pub. Co., 1957). Vol. I.

Wuest, Kenneth S., *Bypaths in the Greek Testament* (Grand Rapids: The Eerdmans Pub. Co., 1940).

__*Galatians in the Greek Testament* (Grand Rapids: The Eerdmans Pub. Co., 1948).

CPSIA information can be obtained
at www.ICGtesting.com
Printed in the USA
BVHW090420180122
626430BV00009B/385

9 781637 646922